Isles of the
CARIBBEAN

Prepared by the Special Publications Division
National Geographic Society
Washington, D. C.

Bursts of song ring out on board Sealestial *during one of Antigua's Sailing Week races. In a captain's cap and a pose worthy of Lord Nelson, who sailed these waters some 200 years earlier, owner Michael Papo, a Michigan physician, oversees crew and guests on his 71-foot ketch. For the occasion Dr. Papo brought in friends and relatives, including his accordion-playing cousin Stijepo Granada from Yugoslavia. Steady breezes, good weather, and the charm of the islands bring serious sailors and fun-lovers alike back year after year. Says Dr. Papo, who never misses Sailing Week, "This is the joy of life."*

JODI COBB (ABOVE AND PRECEDING PAGES)

ISLES OF THE CARIBBEAN

Contributing Authors: TOR EIGELAND, MARY ANN HARRELL, CHRISTINE ECKSTROM LEE, CHARLES MCCARRY, BART MCDOWELL

Contributing Photographers: NATHAN BENN, JODI COBB, COTTON COULSON, DONALD J. CRUMP, TOR EIGELAND

Published by
The National Geographic Society
ROBERT E. DOYLE, *President*
MELVIN M. PAYNE, *Chairman of the Board*
GILBERT M. GROSVENOR, *Editor*
MELVILLE BELL GROSVENOR, *Editor Emeritus*

Prepared by
The Special Publications Division
ROBERT L. BREEDEN, *Editor*
DONALD J. CRUMP, *Associate Editor*
PHILIP B. SILCOTT, *Senior Editor*
MARY ANN HARRELL, *Managing Editor*
WILLIAM L. ALLEN, *Picture Editor*
SUEZ B. KEHL, *Art Director*
RON FISHER, MERRILL WINDSOR, *Consulting Editors*
PATRICIA F. FRAKES, JENNIFER C. URQUHART, *Senior Researchers;* ALICE K. JABLONSKY, *Researcher*

Illustrations and Design
JODY BOLT, *Consulting Art Director*
MARIANNE RIGLER KOSZORUS, CINDA ROSE, *Design Assistants*

LESLIE B. ALLEN, TONI EUGENE, MARY ANN HARRELL, CHRISTINE ECKSTROM LEE, TOM MELHAM, CHARLES R. MILLER, *Picture Legends*
JOHN D. GARST, JR., PETER J. BALCH, MARGARET DEANE GRAY, PATRICIA J. KING, MARK SEIDLER, *Map Research, Design, and Production*

Engraving, Printing, and Product Manufacture
ROBERT W. MESSER, *Manager*
GEORGE V. WHITE, *Production Manager*
JUNE L. GRAHAM, RICHARD A. MCCLURE, RAJA D. MURSHED, CHRISTINE A. ROBERTS, *Assistant Production Managers*
DAVID V. SHOWERS, *Production Assistant*

DEBRA A. ANTONINI, BARBARA BRICKS, JANE H. BUXTON, MARY ELIZABETH DAVIS, ROSAMUND GARNER, NANCY J. HARVEY, SUZANNE J. JACOBSON, CLEO PETROFF, KATHERYN M. SLOCUM, SUZANNE VENINO, *Staff Assistants*

ANNE K. MCCAIN, *Index*

Pages 2-3: The yacht Sirocco *runs northward past landmarks of St. Lucia's coast, the Pitons. Page 1: A girl of Martinique wears beauty marks of glitter on her lips for Carnival. Endpapers: Children rollick at a Martinique beach. Bookbinding:* Sirocco *under sail.*

4

Foreword

To me, the Caribbean is not so much a place as it is a feeling. For among those islands Columbus called the Indies, the pace is languid, the mood tranquil. Here the softness of the air induces the islander to go unhurried, and at once bids the stranger to relax. So it was for Columbus, too, struck as he was by "these lands . . . so fair and so verdant and full of trees and palms." The islands reminded him of springtime in Valencia, Spain. And well they might, for here exists the perpetual warmth of springtime where blossoms follow myriad blossoms, where the brilliance of the stars at night is matched only by the clarity of the waters by day. Indeed, sailboats sometimes seem to rest upon their own shadows in pale green and blue shallows.

For centuries, these islands have been blessed with a natural charm, a quiet, subtle magnetism. Over time, the islanders added their own enhancing touches. There is something enchanting about the sound of a distant steel band drifting across the waters at night. The sea itself seems to keep rhythm, sweeping on and off beaches white in the moonlight.

Ironically, the idyllic world that so moved Columbus was tarnished by many of those who followed him. The seas became a chessboard for warring European powers; the islands became their pawns. Spain, France, England, Denmark, Sweden, the Netherlands all came, and all left their imprint. In the 17th and 18th centuries, some islands changed hands a dozen times or more.

Privateers and pirates sailed, fought, and took refuge here—men like Hawkins and Drake, Blackbeard and Captain Kidd. Reports of their exploits became widespread, and remain part of island lore. One such account held that Blackbeard marooned a mutinous crew on a tiny, lonely cay in the British Virgin Islands, called Dead Chest. The story is thought to have inspired Robert Louis Stevenson to write in *Treasure Island*: "Fifteen men on the dead man's chest—yo-ho-ho, and a bottle of rum!"

Within a century after Columbus's voyages, Europeans had brought thousands of slaves from Africa to sell, and to work the fertile fields of volcanic soil. For a time, the West Indies was one of the world's biggest slave markets.

Gone now are the men-of-war and the pirates. But descendants of those first imported Africans remain, and so do social and economic frustrations not too different from those their forebears knew. Yet the plantation economy that brought slaves to the Caribbean has been changing. New attitudes stir within the islands as surely as the trade winds refresh them. For many islanders the trades must evoke an exhilarating sense of freedom. They symbolize long-dreamed-of recognition, equality, and independence; and for some, no doubt, they instill a desire to enjoy more fully the beauty of their island home.

No matter what the past has inflicted on this very special region of the world, no matter what unrest and uncertainty it faces now, the charm it possessed for Columbus—and for others who have come to know the West Indies through the years—will persist. These will remain among the most treasured islands in the world.

ROBERT L. BREEDEN
Editor, Special Publications Division

Introduction

"If all you want is sun and sea and sand, and drums and rums, you'll find one island very much like another." As a recognized expert on the Caribbean, Professor Sidney W. Mintz of the Johns Hopkins University offers this summary after thirty years' experience. "But," he goes on, "if you begin to meet the people, you'll find striking differences from island to island—from Trinidad to Barbados, or Martinique to Guadeloupe. The better you know them, the more different they become."

Those of us preparing this book have discovered the truth of his words. I met a Vincentian who spoke of his homeland's beauty with enthusiastic pride: "Oh, you really should see it!" I thought of him when I heard of its volcano's disastrous eruption in April 1979, and months later when I heard that its damaged land was green and productive again. One individual's patriotism had made that island unforgettable, distinctive among its sister isles.

"There's such a thing as the Caribbean personality—I believe that," a distinguished West Indian man of letters told me. "We've all known colonial domination. And the climate gives us all one kind of life: an intimate, face-to-face life in the sun, a dramatic life in the open—like life in ancient Greece. But, again as in Greece, our differences are important to us. Many of the world's borders are artificial, political; but islands give you *real* boundaries."

Of course, the Caribbean world includes mainlands as well as islands. Venezuela and Guyana, for example, are members of the Caribbean Conservation Association, a group working to preserve the beauty of the region. It tries, for instance, to coordinate measures for dealing with a major oil spill. And I heard its president, John A. Connell, address an audience full of children; he made it clear that their environment includes a unique cultural heritage as well as the unspoiled air and sea.

That heritage stems in part from the Indians—the courteous Arawak and the formidable Carib—who met the first explorers from Europe; but conquest and disease have left only a few Caribs to survive in the islands.

Europe's cultural bequests are as obvious as the tropical flowers and sunsets, and it is easy to see why some islands changed hands so often—why Guadeloupe in the 18th century might have seemed more valuable to Great Britain or France than Canada. Sugar in that age was like petroleum today: a luxury-turned-commercial-necessity, a source of enormous wealth. And when other regions could supply cheaper sugar, from cane or from beets, the Caribbean lost its old colonial importance.

Now its long-disputed colonies are taking their place among the nations, and entering an age of discovering themselves: a quest as stirring as the search for gold, as dramatic as any clash of galleons. I recognized it in a painting by my new friend Timothy Callender. This canvas shows an idyllic scene, of ships with full white sails in a tropical harbor. Each mainsail has its emblem, a black star. As Timothy confirmed, the star evokes a dream—a vision of ships linking the West Indies and Africa on a course shaped by the trade winds.

One of the Caribbean's heroes planned just such a shipping company—using steamships, of course—in the early 20th century. This was Marcus Garvey, who was born in Jamaica, worked in Harlem, and died in London. His Black Star Line went bankrupt; but his vision lived, one source of the ideal familiar today as Black Pride. Charles McCarry has summed up the spirit apparent in Timothy's work: a mood of "vibrant self-respect." Painters, sculptors, writers, dancers, musicians—artists and their audiences in the islands find this spirit a new inspiration.

Garvey's plan made New York a port of call for his ships because he took it for granted that the United States would continue to play a major role in Caribbean affairs. Something more than a distant alien power, it has been a prospect of opportunity. For generations, people of the islands have left them to look for better fortunes, and many have come north.

"Our people have the North American vision," an island Prime Minister told me. "Everyone has friends and relatives in the States or Canada, and that fact shapes our concept of a proper standard of living." Meanwhile, more and more visitors from the north seek out the loveliness of the Caribbean—a fact that brings some complications with it.

One islander's wry comment gives an example: "All the hotel people tell me, tourists won't eat anything but North American food. And all the tourists I meet ask me, 'Where can we get good Caribbean cooking?' " That struck me because I had already found some: pungent pepperpot stew and luscious nutmeg ice cream.

Yet the point goes beyond comedy. The Caribbean Tourism Research and Development Centre has taken on the task of finding out, for instance, how much of the money that tourists spend will drain right out of the islands to buy American steaks or European wines: Estimates range from 40 to 70 percent. Its director, Jean Holder, told me, "We know that we must rely on tourism to help with development, but we know that it isn't a simple matter at any level—from the national balance of payments to individual encounters." And I remembered the strikingly handsome fruit vendor who told me how strangers would aim a camera at her without even a greeting—"like you a monkey! It's no manners at all!"

Good manners, however casual, are keenly prized in small societies where all the people are well known to each other. Our staff member Jennifer Urquhart noted an essential point in Dominica's capital, Roseau: "It's wonderful for someone from Washington, D. C., with its immense bureaucratic jungle, to sit on a flower-sheltered balcony and have half a country's top officials stroll by and pause for a chat." A nation on this scale may seem too small to succeed in the contemporary world; and some very thoughtful people have questioned the value of the "mini-state," let alone its future.

But I remember a region of enduring beauty, of small islands with limited resources, of minor independent states full of ideals and restlessness and squabbles: What good could come of it? To name only one thing, democracy. It was the little free city-states that gave the world "the glory that was Greece," a standard we still use to measure a free civilization.

The contemporary Caribbean has much in common with ancient Hellas— its sense of community in sports and art and religion. And the Caribbean has one thing infinitely better—unlike ancient Greece, it has escaped from acceptance of human slavery.

Now its statesmen and its athletes, its seafarers and its dramatists, and all its citizens are seeking new dimensions of freedom. If they secure for themselves lives as happy as the good days they have offered so many visitors, none of the friends they have made could wish them better fortune.

MARY ANN HARRELL
Managing Editor

Hispaniola

Puerto Rico

Contents

Aruba

Curaçao

Bonaire

SOUTH AMERICA

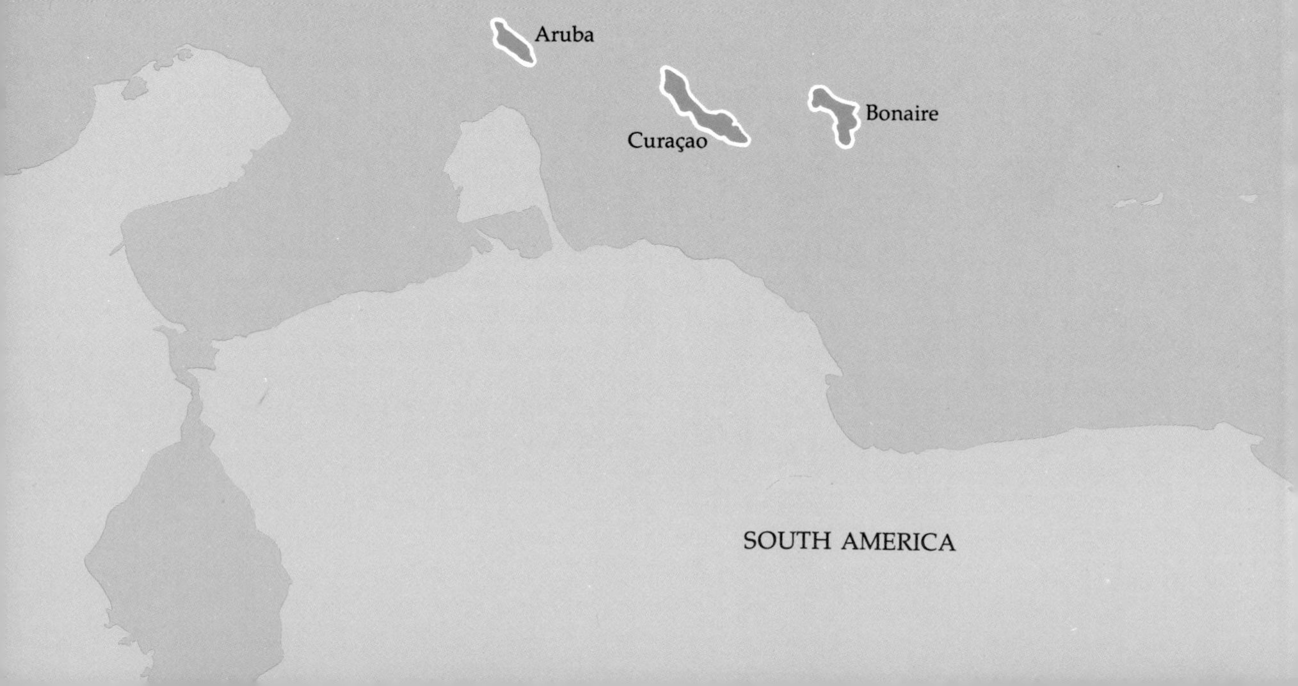

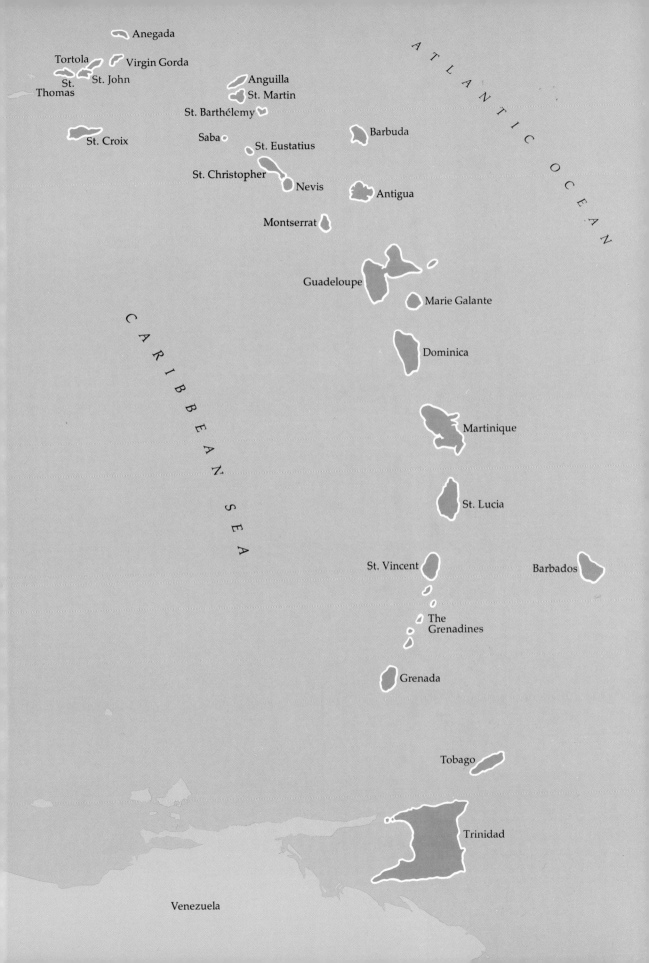

1 | Trinidad and Tobago

Written and photographed by Tor Eigeland

Copper clouds streak a fiery sunset over the Gulf of Paria and west coast of Trinidad, southernmost island in the Caribbean Sea. With Venezuela as close as nine miles, Trinidad once formed part of that mainland and shares with it a geology rich in oil and natural gas. In 1962, Trinidad and the small agricultural island of Tobago to the north combined their diverse histories, peoples, and cultures in a single independent nation.

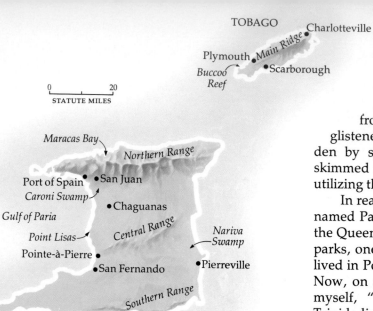

TOBAGO

Charlotteville

Plymouth · *Main Ridge*

Buccoo · Scarborough
Reef

STATUTE MILES
0   20

Maracas Bay

Northern Range

Port of Spain · San Juan
Caroni Swamp

Gulf of Paria

· Chaguanas

Point Lisas · *Central Range*

Pointe-à-Pierre

· San Fernando

Nariva Swamp

· Pierreville

Southern Range

TRINIDAD

"Together We Aspire: Together We Achieve"—their national motto binds Trinidad and Tobago. Similar in climate, with tropical warmth tempered by trade winds, the two islands represent dissimilar environments and life-styles. Trinidad's expanding petroleum industry—the nation's greatest revenue producer— stimulates rapid growth. Tobagonians subsist on small farms in a tranquil land without a single factory. Dominated by the Main Ridge, Tobago's generally uneven terrain offers scanty mineral resources, but unspoiled beaches encourage tourism. Three mountain ranges, a continuation of the Venezuelan cordillera, score Trinidad. From the dense forests of the rugged Northern Range, the land slopes down to canefields and savannahs; hills surround the Central Range, then flatten into rolling plains that yield to highlands in the south.

A t dawn I looked down into Paradise. Wet from early rain, grass and trees glistened in the sun. Racehorses ridden by stableboys in dazzling colors skimmed past men in jogging suits, all utilizing the morning's coolness.

In reality, part of a sugar plantation named Paradise had long since become the Queen's Park Savannah, loveliest of parks, one of my favorite places when I lived in Port of Spain twenty years ago. Now, on a hotel balcony, I was asking myself, "Wha' happenin' an' t'ing?" Trinidadians add this "and thing" to show informality and ease and warmth among equals—an island ideal.

Through yellow poui trees in full golden bloom, I could glimpse stately old wooden mansions trimmed with fretwork. Beyond them spread the city's typical red roofs of tile or painted metal. Then came a startling alteration of the skyline I remembered: new gleaming office buildings of downtown. On the horizon to my right lay the shores of Venezuela, clearly visible.

A sudden tropical shower blurred the continent. Then a brilliant rainbow appeared. Its perfect arc began over the residence of Prime Minister Eric Williams and ended shimmering in the middle of the Savannah.

No, I thought with relief, this country had not lost its magic.

For years I had dreamed of a return, and my dream had almost shattered on arrival. The barnlike airport terminal seemed too small; long lines at passport control seemed not to move. Traffic to Port of Spain was a two-lane high-beam nightmare even at midnight.

The treasury of Trinidad and Tobago is full of oil money. Industrial estates and housing developments have devoured much of the fine farmland outside the major cities. Peering into the roadside darkness, I saw few of the canefields and palms that I remembered.

With nostalgia, I set out through the Savannah in late afternoon to find a coconut vendor. The first one I met, a skinny old East Indian in faded blue denim, greeted me: "Eh-eh, wha' happenin', man?" I ordered a coconut: "Medium, please." Medium means that the nut has some soft jelly—it is not all coconut water.

A deft swipe of a cutlass (as West Indians call a machete) sent the top of the green nut flying. I turned the hull up and drained it: my favorite drink. When I handed the hull back to the vendor, he split it with one whack. Another chop removed a little green wedge of husk, used to scoop out the delicious jelly. Two or three of these nuts are a meal in themselves and, according to Trinidadians, coconut water will cure anything that may be wrong with you.

At dusk more people were out jogging. I saw very few women, but the men included Africans (the modern Trinidad term for black), whites, several Chinese, an Indian, young, old, "t'ick an' t'in" and everything in between.

Schoolgirls in uniform were practicing field hockey, white-clad men were playing cricket, two boys and an older man were trying to fly kites without the benefit of wind, and empty grandstands were waiting for more exciting events—horse races, or the upcoming Carnival.

At a street corner, thirty or forty schoolchildren, most of them black, were trying to hitch a ride home. For weeks, all over Trinidad and Tobago, I would see children out at dawn, trying to get to school, or at sundown, trying to get back home. Twenty years ago there was a lack of schools. Now there was a lack of transportation too.

Lights flickered on in the old section called Belmont. Adults were home from work; they had taken their showers, if the water was running, and were sitting on the verandas of their little pastel-painted wooden houses, cooling off in the delectable tropical night. And *blasting* the year's calypso or steel-band hits from radios or stereo sets.

That night I heard Tobagonian Calypso Rose, Calypso Queen of the World, letting her audience have it at a concert in the Queen's Hall. One of her songs goes like this: *"Ah can't take this tension / Is too much to mention / Port of Spain too small / For this Carnival. . . ."* It expresses the mood that I found.

Calypso often conveys in a few words forceful messages that an expert would have trouble expressing, messages not fully understood by outsiders. That "tension" is hard to explain, but anyone living in Trinidad would know what she meant. Added to the happy pre-Carnival excitement I remembered so well, there is a disturbing new energy in the air.

From old friends and new acquaintances, I learned some of the topics current on small verandas and elegant patios: Carnival or, in descending order, cricket, the skyrocketing cost of living, the terrible state of the roads and postal service and telephone system, the lack of water. These last complications stem from a vastly increased number of customers, especially in the cities. A current song summed it up in popular idiom: "All of we in trouble."

Friends referred me to Rocky McCollin of Radio Trinidad as the man to tell me of calypso. An African with a smoky voice, a good-looking man about 40, he was full of enthusiasm.

"Calypso has a real powerful history. It started from West Africans during the times of slavery. You know, they came from different tribes and had different languages. On the plantation—when the master was there—well, he couldn't understand what they were saying. They used to sing on the guy: 'The mastah big white ugly man. . . .' And it all began like that.

"The calypso—it used to be sung in patois, kind of a French dialect. A calypsonian began to sing in English in 1883, and over the years it has developed. And the upper class, society, never accepted it."

Rocky defined *(Continued on page 20)*

Port of Spain's playground, the Queen's Park Savannah hugs the northern edge of Trinidad's capital between crowded blocks and the modest houses clustered on the slopes of the Belmont Hills. In the shadow of the Northern Range, the multistory Trinidad Hilton commands a broad view of the grandstand, cricket grounds, soccer fields, and racetracks that lace these 200 grassy acres and provide a pastoral escape for Port of Spain's citizens, now more than 60,000. Early-morning haze bathes the hillsides as exercise boys take Thoroughbreds around one of the racecourses. Throughout the Caribbean, horse racing attracts an avid following: Tobago enjoys its own track, while Trinidad boasts three.

*S*miling, Cyrila Henderson and Krishna Gangadeen, a neighbor, welcome visitors to
her weathered home in Mafeking. Rural poverty exists throughout eastern Trinidad,
where stilts raise houses above floodwater levels, and, incidentally, allow shelter for pets
and livestock. Supported by petroleum and manufacturing, urbanization increases on the
island, particularly in the west. On market Saturday in Chaguanas, one of the fast-
growing towns, Sunday's lunch tips the scale. Fifteen miles south, Texaco's refinery
complex at Pointe-à-Pierre sprawls over four square miles and employs 5,000 workers.

Faces of Trinidad reflect a cosmopolitan past—and present. Europeans colonized the island, then imported African slaves to work their sugar plantations. After Britain abolished slavery, contract laborers from India immigrated by the thousand; some also came from China. Now these ethnic strains coexist or mingle. Jan Beausoleil, a secretary, leans from a beach-house porch at Maracas Bay. Trinidadians born (below, left to right), Lystra Cudjoe models and manages a shop; Indira Maharaj-Gobin works as a dental nurse; Nicole Beaubrun studies law. Arlette Johnson (bottom, left), graphic designer, and Meiling Esau, fashion designer, share an Oriental heritage.

Twilight brings a flock of scarlet ibises to roost in a stand of mangroves at the Caroni Bird Sanctuary. Also known as flamants, from the French for "flaming," Trinidad's

the role of the calypsonian today: "He is a poet, a philosopher, and he's the mouthpiece of the people. He is a social commentator. Years ago, they used to sing if the government do wrong, they would attack it. He's free to do that now. My government accepts that."

Fully independent since 1962, this two-island nation has been a republic since 1976. With commercial oil produc-

tion dating from 1908, it is rich as Caribbean countries go. Its population, about 1,200,000, has a complexity unmatched in the islands. Descendants of two ethnic groups, African slaves and East Indian indentured laborers, account for 83 percent. "Dougla" refers to someone half Indian, half black; you also hear "he kinda Portugee," "she kinda white." There are dollops of whites (1.2 per-

national birds flourish in these 437 acres of swamp established as a preserve in 1952. A top tourist attraction, the refuge lies only three miles from downtown Port of Spain.

cent), Chinese (0.9), and others including the Lebanese/Syrian group (0.8); these tiny minorities control a good deal of the country's private wealth.

In religion, you find variation too: Roman Catholic (35.6), Anglican (18.1), Hindu (24.7), Muslim (6.3), Presbyterian (4.2), and "other" (11.1). "Other" includes groups of African inspiration, such as Shango, Rada, and the Spir-

itual Baptists, the so-called "Shouters."

Icacos, Tunapuna, Monos, St. Joseph (San José de Oruña), Pierreville, Redhead, Mafeking, Fyzabad—Trinidad place-names picked out of a hat, all evoking the peoples of the past.

Icacos and some other Amerindian names have survived as the only obvious traces of vanished cultures, though a few racially mixed descendants of the Amerindians can still be found.

Iëre, meaning Land of the Hummingbird in Arawak, was spotted on the horizon by Columbus in 1498. Three peaks of the Southern Range presumably inspired him to name La Ysla de la Trinidad, Isle of the Trinity. He thought the Garden of Eden might be nearby—but he never returned.

Rumors of masses of gold, the Golden King in the Land of Gold, the legends of El Dorado somewhere on the Orinoco attracted Spanish adventurers over the years. Trinidad was a natural base for their quests for El Dorado. In the 17th century a few settlers began growing tobacco or cacao. Eventually, in 1776, the Spaniards invited foreigners from other islands to come and settle—provided that they were Roman Catholic.

In twenty years the population rose from three and a half to almost eighteen thousand. Most of the new colonists were French, from islands to the north, fleeing the upheavals inspired by the French Revolution. Their slaves were seeking *la liberté.*

In 1797 Trinidad was captured by the British. They found on their hands a sugar colony with Spanish laws and a largely French culture as well as practically anonymous black subcultures. By now half the people were slaves.

Trinidad's famous novelist V. S. Naipaul writes of the latter in *The Loss of El Dorado.* His account may shed light on today's Carnival and a tendency to let play-acting spill over into real life. He tells of an "underground life of fantasy," how the Africans had developed their own world "of power and prettiness, of titles, flags and uniforms, kings and queens and courtiers. The planter, looking at his Negroes and seeing only Negroes, never knew. . . ." Naipaul describes a planter, Mr. de Gannes de la Chancellerie, watching Negro women dancing to a patois song. " *'Pain c'est viande béqué,'* the women sang. . . .

Vin c'est sang béqué.
San Domingo!

Nous va boire sang béqué.
San Domingo!
'Bread is white man flesh; wine is white man blood. We going to drink. . . .' It was an old song, from another island. Mr de Gannes didn't take it personally."

It was his blood they meant to drink.

In the end, fantasy and reality blurred. The slaves spoke openly of their plans; the authorities, forewarned, struck first. "They got King Noel, the carter, that night; they got the Negro called the Congo King . . . they got a number of queens and princesses, dauphins and dauphines."

Britain abolished slavery in 1834. Africans in droves abandoned the sugar estates. To replace them, indentured workers were brought from India, about 145,000 in all from 1845 to 1917. Most of them fulfilled their contracts and stayed, accepting the offer of five acres of free land. Today, very roughly speaking, most of the rural population is Indian, and the Africans dominate the cities.

Also African-dominated is the ruling party, the People's National Movement (PNM) founded in 1956 by the brilliant, Oxford-educated Dr. Eric Williams. A controversial, sometimes contentious man, one of the few West Indian leaders who have not come up from the labor movement, he has led his country as Prime Minister since 1962.

Today several factors work against stability: discontent with the aging regime, frustration that national wealth has not brought better public services. I heard of a flight of capital, and of talented people. Finally, a demographic turning point has been reached: East Indians are starting to outnumber the Africans, and in a democratic country want appropriate political power. Pessimists wonder what the outcome will be.

Dr. Roy Neehall, the General Secretary of the Caribbean Conference of Churches, an East Indian of high distinction, is optimistic. I asked if he expected a clash between the two communities.

"No, I don't see that as being possible at all; and if any leader ever attempted to stimulate that kind of thing, I think he would either be shut up or removed very quickly."

I asked how he thought the republic would fare without oil.

"I think we would be in a tragic state," he answered. "I think that because the opposition was drawn largely from the agricultural sector, the government has almost deliberately allowed agriculture to go to the dogs."

Driving about the island, I saw its familiar variations and its new developments. Straight from the traffic jams of Port of Spain I entered the Caroni Swamp, sanctuary for ibises and herons and egrets. When bureaucracy bogged me down, I headed north to my ideal beach—at Maracas Bay, where afternoon light sends the shadows of coconut palms across the white sands into the water.

I passed sleek new suburbs and fading little frame houses on stilts and big old-fashioned houses with wide verandas. Winding bumpy roads led me through lush forests to good-humored villages, to rocky cliffs in the far northeast, to creaky ferries over lazy streams. I heard resort developers talking of golf courses, fishermen still talking of shillings and pence. I caught pungent whiffs of curry, and of Atlantic spray.

On the western plains I saw canecutters at their sweaty work. Sugar is still a major source of jobs, but it no longer rules the economy.

In the lovely valleys of the rugged Northern Range, I saw coffee-and-cacao plantations. My first real homemade coffee was delicious, but many of the old estate dwellings had a derelict air. Even the most weather-beaten villages around the island seemed rich in fruit: citrus, papaya, breadfruit, bananas, many varieties of mangos.

Trinidad has a resource rare in a hungry region: unused fertile land. Still, the republic spends almost twice as much on imported foods as it earns on exported foods. Without oil sales to the U. S., its balance-of-trade surplus would be a deficit of hundreds of millions, in its own or U. S. dollars.

I asked the affable young Minister of Energy and Energy-based Industries, Mr. Errol Mahabir, about a future without oil. After a pause, he said: "Ho! We would go through a very difficult period—extremely difficult!" He reviewed current production of crude, nearly 245,000 barrels a day, and possible reserves of 1,200,000,000 barrels. Exploration has identified large natural-gas fields. "So our future lies mainly in gas." He outlined plans for a fertilizer plant using natural gas, methanol plants, ironworks, an aluminum smelter.

With final costs running into billions, these are part of the Point Lisas Industrial Estate taking shape between Port of Spain and the second largest city, San Fernando. The government hopes these high-technology ventures will create spin-off industries to relieve unemployment, officially estimated at 12 percent in 1979.

As Point Lisas indicates, Trinidad and Tobago ranks as a giant in CARICOM, the 12-member Caribbean Community and Common Market. It has granted substantial loans to poorer and less developed partners, sent them emergency aid after natural calamities.

Petrodollar wealth has also helped at home. It buys a period of grace for solving internal problems, a luxury denied to most of the country's neighbors.

A special time of grace is Carnival. I discussed this with Albert Bailey, of African descent, a great costume designer and mas'-band leader. (Mas' means masquerade.) "Of course," he said in his soft-spoken way, "it helps every year. If we were stuck with this heat [tension], this island would explode. It helps break that tension—it is one big burst of happiness!" He added: "The amount of color we use—we can harmonize the world with color!"   (Continued on page 28)   23

*C*elebrating spring, an East Indian chorus sways and chants to the beat of drums and cymbals during the Hindu religious festival called Phagwa in San Juan, Trinidad. Wearing pink and red to symbolize joy, revelers mark the beginning of their new year by sprinkling one another with red water, or **abeer**, and colored powders (right).

Through their religion, Trinidad's Hindus, a quarter of the population, seek to retain and strengthen their culture. Light reflected from her sequined veil spangles Bhamini Maharaj; clad in red, a traditional color for Hindu brides, she exchanges vows with Bramadath Sharma under a flowered canopy in the temple at El Socorro, near Port of Spain.

F eathery coconut palms and dense mangrove thickets cloak the banks of the Nariva
River as it reaches the sea on Trinidad's east coast. Local men fish with the hand seine,
primarily to feed their own families; they sell any surplus to friends or to visitors at nearby

beaches. Traditional fishing methods survive on both islands, where many small landowners hold a variety of jobs to supplement their incomes. Attempting to reduce expensive imports of fish from North America and Europe, the nation strives to increase its catch.

I took up the same issue with the Reverend Gerard Pantin, a leader in two volunteer foundations that foster self-reliance among the poor. He spoke of Carnival with fervor, as a time when anything goes—and everything goes well. "Every year it is a small miracle. There's a social inversion. For four or five days the poor man is king and the upper class has to take a back seat; big air-conditioned cars have to pull aside for the steel bands. It is a very healthy thing.

"Maybe it's a little make-believe, but we need a little bit of make-believe in our lives, particularly if our lives are poverty-stricken."

For weeks, as part of the buildup, there are jump-ups—parties where dancers literally jump into the air with total abandon, arms outstretched, eyes

*T*hrough a rain of golden petals, an Indian woman in sari and veil strolls near the village of Pierreville. Dropping its blooms after only a few days, the yellow poui usually flowers more than once; local lore holds that the rainy season will not start till it has blossomed three times.
Above, a blue tanager and a black-and-yellow bananaquit share a twig of bougainvillea. On Trinidad and Tobago nest 300 species of birds, far more than on other Caribbean islands that lie farther from the mainland.

half-closed. The haunting, driving, intoxicating Trinidad beat is always there with you, as is the fine rum.

There are also visits to the "pan-yards" where the steel bands practice before the big Carnival parades.

With Scofield Pilgrim, a well-known musician, I went to hear the "Despers," the Gay Desperados. We climbed Laventille, a hill landmark, to a tough neighborhood that used to be even tougher, perhaps because it was poorer, when I lived in Port of Spain. Flowers scented the air; the music, louder and louder, was "sweet"—the pans in tune, the band playing well.

Lit by a full tropical moon and a few dim lightbulbs, seated on two tiers of steel scaffolding, about eighty men were playing as many as nine pans apiece. Conga and bongo drums hit the basic beats. Boys and girls stood by, sometimes pitching in; a boy of eight or nine was playing the bongo drums with great intensity. All seemed relaxed, confident, and absorbed.

Hundreds of people were standing, leaning, sitting around—listening, sucking oranges, smoking, having a beer or drinking rum.

Scofield said of the audience: "They don't miss a beat. If there's a wrong note someone will tell the pan-men about it. Basically, this is the community center. This is *their* band."

A bystander spoke up: "Dese guys—even wid a hundred men—dey doan' make a mistake. Dey all come down TOGEDDER. Dese steel band can play anyt'ing de London Symphony can play. Jus' give dem de melody and dey will learn it. An' dey will play *perfeck!*"

Dey all come down TOGEDDER on jouvet *(jour ouvert)*, Carnival Monday morning. Long before dawn the hills around Port of Spain reverberate with the beating of pan, drowning out the startled roosters to whom this hour belongs. From everywhere people are coming down the road, in costume or not, alone or in groups, some pushing

*H*er smile nearly as wide as her hair ribbon, Ayanna Narine attends a nursery class at Briggs Preparatory School in Port of Spain. On Tobago, older students pass Plymouth's tiny post office. Officials endeavor to expand school facilities and programs for the nation's youth— the more than one-third of its population under 15. At Diego Martin Junior Secondary School, steel-drum practice fascinates a class. Originally an art of the poor, steel-band music has gained popularity and respect. Trinidadians devised their first "pans" from surplus oil drums after World War II, then perfected rhythms the world now enjoys. Cricket, the nation's most popular sport, appeals to everyone: Wielding a bat, a young fan dreams of glory.

their pans on wheels for miles, all descending on downtown Port of Spain. Many come from all-night parties.

Shiff-shiff-shiff-shiff—the unforgettable insistent sound of thousands of shuffling feet following their musicians. Even if the drums should stop for a moment there is still the rhythmic shiff-shiff-shiff.

With Port of Spain as focal point, the country explodes in a two-day frenzy of dazzling color, fun, fantasy—a bacchanal, as Trinidadians say.

Dragons, Vikings, knights—a thousand creations parade across the stage of the Savannah. Each mas' band, some with thousands of marchers, has its theme. Some of the old spontaneity has given way to professional design, while the steel bands have become much more sophisticated.

Watching the mas' bands bounce, slide, jump, and shuffle by, I decided that I had misjudged the scope of the arts here. I had thought of writers like Naipaul and Samuel Selvon, painters-and-dancers like Boscoe and Geoffrey Holder, painters Alladin and Noel Vaucrosson, and Beryl McBurnie, the indomitable queen of national dance. I had forgotten Carnival. Carnival is art, even if its brilliant creations live only a few glorious hours.

Deeply remote, yet on the same island, there exists another world. In a year's residence I never felt that I had entered the life of the East Indian community. Its ritual strikes the outsider, of course. By chance one Sunday at a river in the northeast, I saw a white-robed pandit presiding while five Hindu men, half-immersed in the clear waters, shaved the heads of five others. This is done as a token of respect, the pandit told me, ten days after the death of an older man.

Nothing has given me a keener sense of this world than a poem by Derek Walcott, a St. Lucian by birth but a long-time resident of Trinidad. "The Saddhu of Couva" is the lament of an aged ascetic in an Indian-dominated town, with firms like Ramlochan's car repairs: "There are no more elders. / Is only old people." At sunset the Saddhu sees his own soul "like a white cattle bird" flying "over the ocean of the evening canes . . . because, for my spirit, India is too far."

Distance for the spirit. From Trinidad to Tobago, only 20 miles. But a different life. Free of the tensions of Trinidad, Tobago is only one-sixteenth the size. The population is less than 40,000, nearly all African by descent.

"Exotic Trinidad and tranquil Tobago," said Junia Browne of the Tourist Board in a good Tourist Board phrase. Grinning, he added: "The Beatles came here and walked down the streets unmolested."

From twenty years earlier I recalled an idyllic blur of sun, sand, sea, coconut palms, and beaches. Now I saw more of the magnificent beaches and the famous Buccoo Reef, a coral reef where the rainbow no doubt pilfered its colors. I drove on mountain trails through exuberant tropical foliage, and through the undulating flatlands of the southwest. I visited the tiny, charming capital city of Scarborough. It is all very accessible.

Friendly, polite, not quite so accessible are the Tobagonians. They give a clear impression of dignified strength, and I heard a legend that conveys something of their character.

On the northwestern coast is a spot called Ma Rose Point. Ma Rose, an old and kindly woman, was an Ibo slave on the Charlotteville estate. Tobagonian slaves were supposed to be a special breed, the pick of the crop, haughty and brave and somewhat troublesome.

One day a white overseer snapped his whip at Ma Rose as she was carrying a heavy bundle of canes on her head. When she stumbled and fell, he still lashed at her. Gathering her strength, she sprang up, hurled him to the ground, and bit into his throat until he died. Next day, when she was about to be tied to a mango tree to be whipped to death as a warning to the rest, she broke away from her burly guards. Singing an Ibo song, a song of the drum dance, she ran for the nearby cliff and threw herself into the sea.

It is said that when the sea is especially rough around this point, Ma Rose is thirsty; the fishermen who row past will throw some rum overboard to calm the waves.

"They are proud," Dr. Lou Lichtveld told me. Surinam-born, a retired Dutch diplomat, at age 76 he looks 60—because he lives in Tobago, he says. "In my opinion, one of the main reasons is that a large part of the population here owns land. Small parcels. They can live; they are not dependent. Nobody goes hungry. Nobody is miserable. When you want some work done, you have to ask for it as a favor.

"Tourism earns quite a lot of money," he told me, but mainly for the owners of the big hotels. "It sets bad examples; people see a luxury without any meaning."

Settled by Arawaks two thousand years ago, then by warlike Caribs, later by the Dutch, Tobago had changed hands 17 times before Britain secured it as a colony in 1814. There was a saying, "rich as a Tobago planter," before sugar prices sagged some decades later. "Now," said Dr. Lichtveld, "you have to look hard to find *one* stalk of cane."

I did meet one of the last few sugar-makers, Mr. Lawrence Charity of Carnbee Village. Life along the road that morning followed daily routine. Boys were walking their goats on leashes, to find browse. At the public water taps, people were washing their faces or filling pails to be "headed" home. As always, schoolchildren were hitching rides and saying, most politely, when they got out, "T'anks very much."

Pink poui trees were in bloom everywhere. Black clouds hung over a steel-gray ocean. Cattle grazed here and there, white egrets always following. Chickens and turkeys roamed near small, pastel-painted wooden houses on stilts. One of these was Mr. Charity's.

An elderly man with a humorous gleam in his eye, he greeted me politely. I was a bit late—at 7:30 a.m. they had nearly finished "juicing" the cane in a little shack with a tiny electric mill. Propped up by rocks outside it was a huge "copper," a boiler with a fire roaring under it.

The four men at work were feeding the fire with dry logs or coconut husks, stirring or skimming the boiling cane juice, and "limin' "—shooting the breeze, teasing and laughing. Sometimes Mr. Charity asserted himself in the Spanish he had learned in Venezuela: *"Dispense Usted, señor—yo soy el capitán aquí* (Excuse me, sir—I'm the captain here)." His radio reported an all-day cricket match from Barbados, West Indians being cricket-mad; birds were singing, hens clucking, the men joking.

"You givin' de young fellas too much worry." *"Me?"* "Yeh—wid de girls. At your age you trouble!" Banter about the rewards of love is a constant diversion in country and city alike.

The whole day passed happily like this. Toward sunset the bubbling syrup turned yellowish-brown and gave off a delicious smell; it was strained through clean cloth into big pans to yield "wet sugar" with a distinctive homemade flavor.

Tobagonians know they have a good and a peaceful life. They resent the Trinidadians, accuse them of crime and corruption, even talk of secession. When we parted, Mr. Charity's final comment was this: "If the gov'ment would pay more attention to the religious people, they would get less trouble, bring the religious-minded to reduce crime. I don't know why they not scrutinizin' the ships and them that come here sufficiently to prevent them from sellin' the revolver here too."

As the morning jet rose over the

33

water, I could see the little open fishing boats pitching and rolling past the Buccoo Reef, out after flying fish. Two days earlier, down there, I had jinxed the luck of a good fisherman; we had come back empty-handed after a long, long day with "a growlin' sea."

Now, within minutes, I was looking down at Trinidad's north coast, to me its most appealing region. Its people are mostly black; its life keeps much of the unchanged dignity of Tobago's.

Ominously, however, some of these northern hills harbor what are locally called "guerrillas"—smugglers, common criminals, and drop-outs, mainly; a few with political axes to grind; men "sellin' the revolver."

A brutal change from Tobago, the airport and Port of Spain area that day was one vast sizzling traffic jam. I struggled through it to a villa just outside the city for a farewell dinner at the home of Owen and Rhona Baptiste.

Owen is editor of the Caribbean monthly magazine *People*. Rhona, now on its staff, was a teacher before she worked for the Caribbean Conference of Churches. She had prepared my favorite Trinidad dishes: a superb callaloo soup, made from dasheen leaves and crabs and secret ingredients (perhaps a sprinkling of grated coconut?); stewed chicken with a subtle sauce fired by drops of the world's hottest pepper-sauce, made in Trinidad; homemade coconut ice cream for dessert.

Owen and Rhona discussed some of my most troublesome questions. Why the outburst of big and small fires, bombings, throwings of Molotov cocktails? A whole downtown block had recently burned to the ground.

"Tor, there is a great deal of mystery surrounding that," said Owen.

"From '70 to '73, there was a lot of crime committed in the name of a group called the National Union of Freedom Fighters. But they were wiped out, right?

"Then there was a spate of robberies and murders that apparently had nothing to do with politics. Since '77 it has seemed that there's a movement—very, very secret—aimed at business mainly; not so much against government, although schools have been burned, and customhouses."

Were any of these cases solved?

Owen stated flatly: "Not one."

What would all this lead to?

"I don't think we have a destination, really," Rhona replied. "We're going along, the entire Caribbean is going along. The ideology, if there is one, is crass materialism. Some years ago we had, at least, religion to offset that—a certain morality. Now, it doesn't matter how you get rich or how you manage to have ten big cars. Once you do it, you become a hero."

I thought of Walcott's Saddhu, who says: "My friends spit on the government./I do not think is just the government./Suppose all the gods too old,/ Suppose they dead and they burning them,/ . . . Suppose all the gods were killed by electric light?"

"You've got to be an optimist to live in Trinidad," Owen had said to me at one point.

A hopeful opinion, my own, is that Trinidad and Tobago has real cause for optimism. This land of tremendous variety has yet to discover its greatest resource: its unique, imaginative, magnificent people. Properly inspired, they could "harmonize the world with color," as Albert Bailey said; and sharing their many assets of wealth from land and sea, they could indeed happily "all come down TOGEDDER!"

Glossy hot syrup strains through burlap in the last phase of sugar-making at Lawrence Charity's home in Tobago's Carnbee Village. Until prices fell in the 1880's, the island's economy depended on sugar; today little cane survives, and few farmers process it.

Carnival

Milling throng of masqueraders, "mas' makers," caps two days of
festivities: The octopus section of the Carnival of the Sea band
parades for judging at Queen's Park Savannah. From dawn
Monday to "las' lap" at midnight Shrove Tuesday, Trinidad
explodes in Carnival. Groups of disguised revelers—some with just
a few members, others with more than 3,000—"jump up" in the
streets to steel-band music and the witty refrains of calypso songs.
Children share the fun. Bright and sturdy tulips bloom in the final
review of junior bands at a Queen's Park grandstand (left).
Following pages: Bearded king of the Universal Festivals band,
"Poseidon in an Evening Gala" straddles a shimmering sea horse.

Billowing scarlet flames lick the queen of the Spectrum band, Juanita Woo Chong as the Cosmic Inferno. Created from plastic, sequins, beads, and cane, an Oriental Magic Dragon—Chinese symbol of good luck—ruled the Hocus Pocus group. Peter Samuel captured the title of King of Carnival for his forceful portrayal of Devil Ray (below). With his malevolent glare and lashing tail, he led Peter Minshall's Carnival of the Sea, 34 sections of masqueraders who won 1979 Band of the Year honors. Undulating eels, brilliant tropical fishes, crashing waves, and even an oil slick twisted through Port of Spain. In early "mas' making," former slaves burlesqued the extravagant pre-Lenten festivities that their masters had brought from European courts. Now, Carnival grows more elaborate and expensive yearly; for these few days, says the author, "the rest of the world does not exist at all."

2 | Three Dutch Islands

Written by Bart McDowell and photographed by Nathan Benn

Roofs of red-orange tile mark the town of Willemstad on Curaçao, largest of the Netherlands Antilles. Beyond an arm of the great harbor called the Schottegat rise the storage tanks of a Royal Dutch Shell oil refinery. With its sister islands Aruba and Bonaire, Curaçao bears a Dutch stamp in a tropical setting. Once the haunt of pirates and slave dealers, the islands today rank among the most prosperous in the Caribbean.

Willemstad seems too wholesome for ghosts. It's the sunlit, oddly Dutch capital of Curaçao and the Netherlands Antilles. Its pastel swatch of waterfront suggests the stage set for a musical comedy.

Yet friends had told me—seriously—a story of my own hotel: "Two men were killed building it, and now they return at night, dressed in black."

"Yes," a Curaçao priest had added, "men can come back."

I cannot be sure of the hotel ghosts; they didn't show up for me. But Willemstad, with all its well-scrubbed looks, is visibly haunted by the past.

Geography explains much in the ABC islands, as Aruba, Bonaire, and Curaçao are called. These are leeward isles, dehydrated by the prevailing northeasterlies just before those trade winds invade South America. Galleons, pirate ships, men-of-war, and yachts have all filled their sails with these fair winds. The great harbor at Willemstad, the Schottegat, has welcomed many a traveler. In 1499 came Alonso de Ojeda and Amerigo Vespucci. Peter Stuyvesant arrived to govern in 1643, lost a leg, and then went on to New Amsterdam. The pageant has continued with adventurers, missionaries, the exiled and shipwrecked, slaves, bureaucrats, smugglers, bankers, oilmen, scuba divers, gamblers. And journalists, like me.

On my first visit since 1953, I noticed some changes. The old hotel where I had stayed had vanished, "burned to the ground in the riots of 1969," as a friend explained. Colonial rule had changed; these islands were now recognized as autonomous components of the Kingdom of the Netherlands. The Shell

Arid outposts of a once-vast trade empire, the so-called ABC islands lie within fifty miles of the coast of Venezuela. A Spanish expedition discovered Curaçao in 1499, and the three remained in Spanish possession until 1634, when a Dutch force routed the local garrison. Initially, the Dutch used Curaçao as a naval base in their war of independence from Spain. Later it became a slave center, where ships from West Africa brought their human cargo. On the site of a plantation called Asiento now stands a refinery of Royal Dutch Shell. Shell opened its plant in 1918 to processs Venezuelan crude for U. S. and European customers.

Among the 240,000 inhabitants of the ABC's, conversation usually runs in the unofficial language Papiamento, a mix of Spanish, Dutch, Portuguese, and English, with some African and Amerindian words. An island author says fondly, "I call it music-language. You can change tone and get a different meaning."

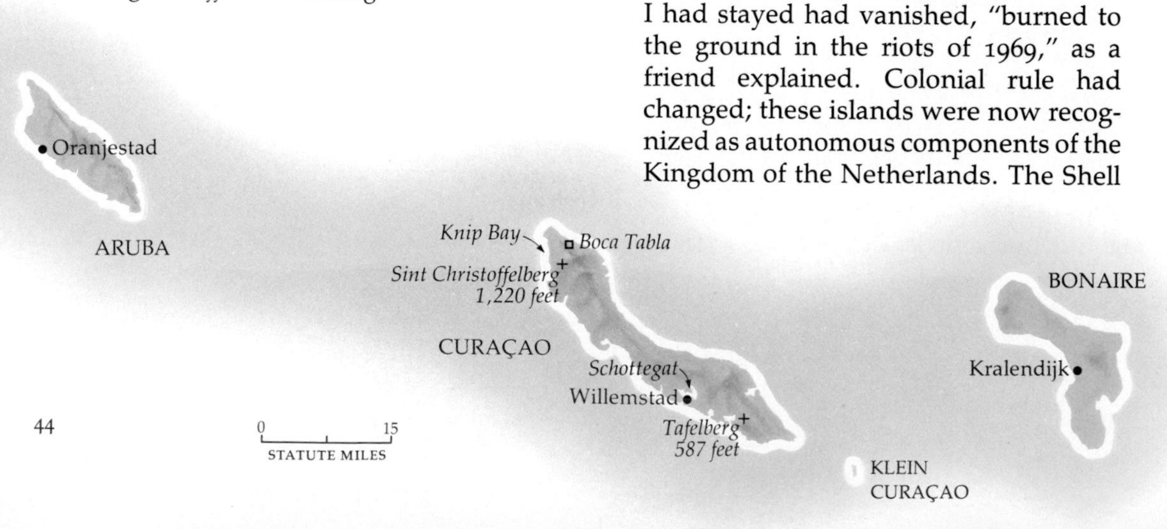

• Oranjestad

ARUBA

Knip Bay ☐ *Boca Tabla*

Sint Christoffelberg⁺
1,220 feet

BONAIRE

CURAÇAO

Kralendijk•

Schottegat
Willemstad •

Tafelberg⁺
587 feet

KLEIN
CURAÇAO

0   15
STATUTE MILES

oil refinery had turned to automation, and hired fewer people than before. Tourism had grown. So had unemployment—at least by estimated statistics.

But these Dutch isles remained among the most prosperous in the West Indies, with an annual per capita income of $1,700 U. S. I still heard Papiamento, a language ("Not a dialect, please!") spoken only among the 240,000 citizens of the ABC's.

People were still overwhelmingly concerned with oil and water. Both are hard to come by, and utterly essential: oil for storage and refining—the major industry—and water for survival. Every drop of tap water is distilled from the sea. As a joke puts it, ignoring Curaçao's namesake liqueur, "We have the only distilleries in the Caribbean that produce only the chaser!"

Yet the salty, crystalline sea provides a special abundance. Wide beaches on Aruba are among the world's whitest. Swimming—even wading— along the coral reefs of Bonaire, I found the most spectacular underwater world I have visited in either hemisphere.

The choppy surface, of course, is the highway for vital activities. From the windows of my haunted hotel, I never tired of watching water traffic.

The 14 anachronistic stories of the Curaçao Plaza rise within the 35-foot-thick walls of the old Waterfort. Sunbathers at the hotel pool bask beside the 18th-century cannon still pointed grimly seaward. Spain, the Netherlands, and Britain—briefly—have occupied these shores; pirates also tried.

Now full, low-lying oil tankers move from the horizon to the harbor entrance. Like a garden gate, the 500-foot pontoon bridge named for Queen Emma gradually swings back against the Otrabanda bank; and through the open channel, tankers, cruise ships, and small craft surge inside.

Oil and clear water seem an unlikely combination. "But we run a clean harbor," says Captain H. Hendrikse, of the Harbor and Pilot Service. "Ship captains actually complain that our water is *too* clean. They say, 'We pump up small crabs with our cooling water.' "

Energy has long been the commercial stuff of Curaçao. When the Panama Canal opened in 1914, Curaçao was the great coaling port for steamers crossing the isthmus. Earlier, when human muscle powered the New World economy, the harbor site of Asiento—the very spot where Shell now refines oil—acquired its name, which means "slave market."

"Physical strength was important for field hands," recalls my friend E.A.V. Jesurun, director of cultural affairs for the Netherlands Antilles and known by everyone as Papy. "Strong slaves were exported. Curaçao has almost no agriculture, and the merchants here didn't want aggressive slaves as house servants. So they chose slaves at least partly for their appearance. The Sephardic Jews especially admired beautiful black girls. Some were taken as mistresses, and the children of mixed blood were sent to school by their fathers. Thus Jews founded our middle class."

Papy sketches this social history with personal pride: "The Jesuruns were Jewish, of course—the Rothschilds of the Caribbean in the 19th century, bankers who even issued their own money." Papy shows off his cuff links made from Jesurun coins, but he is no less proud of his black heritage; without it, he could scarcely have risen to high political positions in the National Party.

"When you go around the island," he says, "you'll see some really beautiful black people—fine features, women with lovely figures." And so I did.

I also noted landscapes remarkably varied for such a small island. In the south, the 587-foot Tafelberg commands a view of a harbor called Spanish Water, where yachts scud about like water bugs, and of the oil terminal of a bay named for the Venezuelan city of Caracas. Tiers precisely level, 40 feet high and intensely white in the tropic sun, mark the sides of this "table mountain," where explosives and giant machines of the Curaçao Mining Company carve away layers of phosphate.

Beyond, the island dwindles green and unused to East Point. Toward the north, where the mountain called Sint Christoffelberg rises almost 1,250 feet, the view blurs into a choppy, rocky, wind-nagged terrain. Curaçao, in fact, reminded me of my native West Texas; some 10,000 short-hair goats overgraze a countryside that bristles with thorns of dry bushes, prickly pear, and a kind of organ cactus called *cadushi*.

And as in Texas, cultures overlap.

One day I made my Willemstad rounds with big Jan Rozier. Like every-

*P*rotective gear shields maintenance man John Samuel Sillcot from inhaling dust when he cleans pipework during a shutdown in the catalytic cracking unit at the Shell plant. At right, inspectors make a last check on the newly cleaned distillation column. Curaçao's largest employer, with 2,680 workers, the refinery can process 362,000 barrels of crude per day.

one in Curaçao, Rozier has a nickname— Sopa, or Soup. He represents a hearty bowlful, a cheerful man both expansive and expanded. He knows everybody.

"You have seen the Bolívar House?" he asks. "No? Well, here it is, right on the sea." In this early 19th-century mansion, now a museum, glass cases hold memorabilia of the great Venezuelan liberator Simón Bolívar, who fled here as a refugee in 1812. Upstairs, from the bedroom windows, a seascape spreads toward Venezuela, forty miles away, source of most of the oil processed at Curaçao's refinery.

"We still get a lot of Venezuelan visitors," says Sopa. "They come, they buy steam irons and TV sets, and make a little business when they go home.

"And our food!" Sopa's smile expands across his round face. "You know our floating market? Our produce comes by boats from the Venezuela coast."

Quite a cornucopia floats in, by diesel more than sail, in the small craft that tie up to a Willemstad quay. Here, in the shade of awnings made of sugar sacks, Curaçao homemakers pinch tomatoes, heft oranges, and pay high prices.

"No, we don't bargain on prices," a floating merchant explained. "After all, it takes us 15 hours to reach the mainland." These traders speak Spanish, even with the customers, for most Curaçaons slip easily back and forth—between Papiamento, Spanish, English, and Dutch.

Recipes have the same ethnic variety. Sopa, who seemed an ample authority, recommended the Golden Star Restaurant, where the crowd was strictly local. I enjoyed a fried fish from Venezuelan waters, then *funchi*, a version of yellow cornmeal mush, molded attractively and dry enough to stand alone.

Indonesian *rijsttafel* is to the Dutch what enchiladas are to Texans. Here you can order a 23-dish rijsttafel. But a dish of local origin was my favorite: *Keshi jena*, meaning stuffed cheese, comes from the custom *(Continued on page 54)*

F acing a daunting routine, workers for the Curaçao Drydock Company pause before resuming their labor—to clean, paint, and repair the 61,074-ton tanker Elektra *within four days. The firm runs the largest commercial drydock in the Western Hemisphere, where 1,000 employees work in three shifts around the clock. While a member of a cleaning crew scours the hull with jets of water (below), mechanics and electricians overhaul the engines. For ships needing minor underwater repairs, the firm employs divers trained in welding.*

*C*radling a velvet-draped Torah, Rabbi
Aaron Peller stands in Willemstad's
Mikve Israel-Emanuel Synagogue. The
local Jewish community dates from the
1650's, when Sephardic Jews came seeking
Dutch tolerance. They helped found other
communities in the New World, sending
money to congregations in Philadelphia,
Charleston, and New York. Their present
temple, dedicated in 1732, remains the
oldest in continual use in the Americas.
Behind the rococo façade of the Penha
House, shoppers find such duty-free goods
as French perfume and Scottish cashmere
sweaters. At a new waterfront market,
Willemstad residents examine baskets of
sweet potatoes, oranges, plantains, and
other produce brought by schooner from
Venezuela. Low, sporadic rainfall severely
handicaps agriculture in the ABC's.

Waterless and barren, the islet of Klein Curaçao supports only a lighthouse and a handful of fishermen's shacks. For smugglers, however, it may serve as a way station for slipping contraband into Venezuela. Before Spain's South American colonies won their independence in the early 19th century, Dutch traders turned a handsome profit with similar tactics. As one islander told the author, "Smuggling is not against our laws."

On the northern side of Curaçao lies Boca Tabla (right), a small and seldom-visited grotto created by wave action in an old coral formation.

of filling the red rind of Dutch cheeses with pork and herbs from the islands. Delicious.

"It's hard to find a kosher keshi jena," reports Rabbi Aaron Peller, "but some of my people make it with fish." He serves Congregation Mikve Israel-Emanuel, founded in 1654 by Sephardic Jews who came from Spain and Portugal seeking Dutch tolerance and peace. They prospered; their townhouses grew tall. Their handsome temple was the largest building in the city when it was dedicated in 1732; it ranks as the oldest in continuous use in the New World.

"When we bless the new month, we do it in five languages," says Rabbi Peller. "And on Yom Kippur we read the Book of Jonah in Papiamento. We sing grace in Spanish, and have a prayer for the royal family in Portuguese."

Hardworking people from the Portuguese island of Madeira supply labor for the Fuik plantation in southeastern Curaçao, unusual in its atmosphere of palm-shaded languor. It has a thousand coconut palms and 26 wells, 8 with windmills, for irrigation. It's a labor-intensive truck farm, with banana and mango orchards as well as eggplants and other vegetables.

"Our best gardeners come from Madeira," a merchant assured me. "And our ice-cream salesmen. And maids for our houses also. Black girls don't like to work as live-in maids; it reminds them of slave days." Island labor specialist J.A.F. Spit says, "With unemployment of 17 to 20 percent, it's still hard to find unskilled workers." And others explained it like this: "People are afraid to fall back into slavery."

No wonder. As a wholesale market for slaves, Curaçao saw its share of suffering, rebellion, and torture.

"To wash away sadness, slaves danced the *tambú*," remarks Elis Juliana. "Do you know it, our drum dance? Now children dance it on TV, but in the old days no *decent* people danced the tambú at an elite party. You do it this way—

your body straight up, completely relaxed." Elis, a 51-year-old black man of wiry build and animation, lifts his weight with one foot and drops it sharply to the other. "See the footsteps. Arms remain relaxed, never lifted up. The whole body is shaking—very important symbolism, and much sourness of slavery to wash away."

As a youth Elis "wrote love poems to girls—in Spanish." Then he turned to the local language. "My first poem in Papiamento was about a duck, 'Patu.' I read it to groups—rhythmically walking like a duck on the stage. Everybody could understand it."

Since the 1960's, Elis Juliana has written 15 books. He now enjoys a successful career as a painter and sculptor. But Papiamento remains an intense interest. "I call it music-language. You can change tone with it and get a different meaning. Grammar is simple."

Vocabulary combines Spanish, Portuguese, Dutch, English, American Indian, "and African words, too," insists Elis, "especially our double words for birds—like *wara-wara*."

Father Paul Brenneker, a scholarly Dutch priest who has lived in the islands forty years, calls the language "very rich." He has taped 1,400 conversations and collected about 5,000 nicknames, "all revealing." His own nickname? He laughs. "Well, I have a daily radio program at half-past twelve. They call me 'Blah-blah of 12:30.'"

Local stations broadcast commercials and news in Papiamento. With rusty Spanish and close attention, I could follow along, but I couldn't spot dialect differences among the islands.

Some of these differences are political. On Aruba, newspaper publisher Jossy Mansur explained that "we favor traditional spelling and people on Curaçao favor phonetic. On Aruba we have adopted an official spelling for our island. And now we have a strong movement for teaching Papiamento in schools. So far, our teachers can't do it—no textbooks or training. Many of our teachers are Dutch."

But with the old Netherlands Empire receding, things are changing. "The Dutch want to get rid of us," several islanders complained. In fact, many Netherlanders would like to be rid of responsibility for their six Antillean islands, the ABC's and the 3-S group some 500 miles to the northeast, Saba, Statia, and Sint Maarten.

Among the ABC's, independence from the Netherlands is no rallying cry: Nationhood brings new expenses of its own. On Aruba, however, independence means something else.

"Historically, Aruba was always a subcolony of Curaçao," says Jossy Mansur. "And now when an industry is established, Curaçao gets it—factories for beer, and paint, and flour. On Aruba, we pay the huge customs duties, but do not get the jobs. And in the Antillean parliament, Curaçao has 12 seats while we have but 8.

"Curaçao is mostly black and orientates itself toward the other black Caribbean islands. We are more mestizo Indian and look toward South America. This isn't race discrimination. Just sentiment. We want to be independent of Curaçao—not of Holland."

Politics aside, I was surprised at the differences the islands present. Rural Aruba seems wilder and wider than Curaçao, yet Aruban hotels are handsomer and served with greater flair. The island gives a sense of expansive modernity, the illusion of having more than its 63,000 people. They represent 43 or 44 nationalities—"We have only one Japanese," I was told, "so when she goes to Curaçao, it changes our statistics."

One of these nationalities is U. S., thanks to the sprawling Exxon refinery on the southeast coast.

"We have 60-odd expatriate families," says economist Gene Goley, but more than 350 staff-management Arubans outnumber executives from the States. Company commissaries have given way to local businesses, and community relations are good.

An oil spill on any of the ABC islands could devastate tourism and other enterprises. So far, no serious spill has occurred. "Partly good luck," said a Dutch marine, "but mostly it's work. We Dutch have some experience working with the sea."

On Bonaire, the success seems greatest. Ten thousand flamingos breed here—one of three great colonies in the New World—and feed in the salty inlets, which get special protection. Near the Goto Meer sanctuary, the Bonaire Petroleum Corporation (BOPEC) serves supertankers up to 500,000 tons deadweight, and stores nearly ten million barrels of oil for transshipment to the U. S. Small craft stand by with vacuum cleaners to slurp up any oil that goes astray, and a floating dam shields the inlet.

"Flamingos are delicious," said my Bonaire companion Arcadio Cicilia, known to everyone as Cai-Cai. "They taste like shrimp. Don't be shocked. I ate flamingo as a boy. We no longer eat them here. Bonaire is conservation-minded now."

Islanders here keep things living, especially within the coral reefs. "We outlawed spearfishing years ago," Cai-Cai told me with sincere pride.

Some of the credit must go to local divers. "We don't horse around with our ocean," says one expatriate resident, an American. "We leave only bubbles and take only memories."

With old tennis shoes for wading—coral is razor sharp and sea urchins are plentiful here—I went out in face mask and snorkel to explore underwater Bonaire, and found it the most beautiful place I know.

It is silent except for the slow rasp of snorkeled breathing. My own. White sunshine bends in the water's moving lens and reflects from white sand. Three white fish, barely visible in their high-key world, (Continued on page 62)

OFICINA
I
GOBIERNO
DI
ARUBA

Anthems to independence inspirit a Flag Day rally at Oranjestad, capital of Aruba. The sponsoring party, the People's Electoral Movement, promotes separation from Curaçao—but not from the Netherlands—and has adopted the unofficial, single-starred flag. Led by Betico Croes (on balcony, third from right), the party has won five of Aruba's eight seats in the Antilles parliament.

Luxury hotels on Aruba cater to North American, Venezuelan, and Dutch tourists, who come for the gambling casinos and the spotless white beaches.

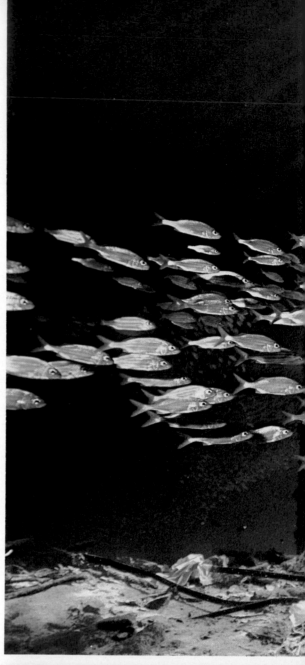

*U*nderwater bonanzas of tropical fish and coral lure divers from around the world to Bonaire, easternmost of the ABC's. After a day of snorkeling, the author called underwater Bonaire "the most beautiful place I know."

Among the Caribbean's most dazzling creatures, the parrotfish (below) crunches coral into fine bits to find the polyp inside. The fish's teeth fuse together to shape its mouth like a parrot's beak.

At right, a school of smallmouth grunts glides past a Bonaire pier. Grunts rarely stray from coral reefs, where they feed at night on shrimp and other crustaceans. On the pilings, featherduster worms (below, center) emerge from sponges and tunicates encrusted there and capture plankton with their spiral-shaped tentacles.

Antennae waving, a pair of barber shrimp lie inside a barrel sponge. Many predatory fish—including moray eels —visit such "cleaning stations," letting them scour gills and mouth for parasites.

Spindly legs trailing, flamingos sail over a Bonaire salt pan. About 10,000 birds live on the island, feeding on small mollusks and brine shrimp. If these become scarce, they take up mud by the billful for the tiny creatures it contains. In the breeding season, they build conical mounds of mud for nests; the female lays a single egg on top.

Since the 1640's, salt-making has proved a mainstay of Bonaire's economy. Seawater dries into crystals in vast evaporating pans before export to U. S. and Caribbean markets. Personnel of the present saltworks, and of Bonaire's petroleum transshipment depot, take great pains to protect the island's ecosystems—especially the easily panicked flamingos.

poise parallel and watch me with round black eyes. I back away and they follow, as if curious.

Seen through a diving mask, my own feet are immense—distance and time have gone surreal. I float, buoyant, toward magnificent antlers of coral, and here I begin to see some of the two thousand species of aquatic life from these undulating waters: small, brilliantly purple fish with saffron foreheads . . . a disk-shaped fish with black polka dots . . . yellow-streaked creatures moving like missiles . . . a warty brown bulldog of a fish works his underslung jaw . . . a paper-thin creature turns at right angle and becomes a plate of electric blue: Matisse on an acid trip.

In this underwater world, nature seems clean, balanced, and enduring.

Even ashore, Bonaire seems a place of harmony. Its ethnic mix includes blacks like Curaçao's and mestizos like Aruba's. As Cai-Cai drives the roads and streets, he waves and honks at friends—especially all the shapely girls. "I am the gardener," he explains gallantly, "and they are the flowers." And Frans Booi, chief of the island's cultural and educational department, says, "We are all from families of pirates!"

On Curaçao, by contrast, race relations have been calm but tentative, as if haunted since May 1969, when a labor dispute turned nasty. "Labor marched, then rioted," a politician recalled. "The police couldn't cope. Then the rioters started fires and the fire department couldn't cope, either. Mostly, drunks did the damage. When they sobered up, many wept." They had cause: Statistics showed 79 injured and 2 dead; the estimates of property damage ranged upward from $35,000,000.

"It really wasn't racial," a merchant insists; and the experience of a young Dutch woman supports him. When rioters stopped her car and ordered her out, she swore at them—in Papiamento. They broke into laughter, shouting "She's one of us!" And let her go.

Nonetheless, the violence awakened many to the need for change. Clubs opened their membership to more people of color. The Crown appointed the first black Governor. Employers trained more local people for jobs formerly held by *macambas*, the Dutch. Political parties reached out for new segments of the population.

From a respectful distance, I watched one campaign. At a rally of the established party faithful, a middle-class family crowd heard tambús played by a ten-piece band. Partisans of other sorts paraded in caravans, streaming crepe paper and enthusiasm. On election night, victory went to a new party of the left; but politics remained essentially neighborly, a matter of personalities and friendships. Naturally: Everyone knows everyone else on these intimate isles.

It reminds me of my visit with Curaçao's Renaissance man, Elis Juliana. He was mounting a new gallery show of his thumbnail-size ink drawings—pictures so small that he furnished magnifying glasses for guests.

"As a boy, I enjoyed looking at ants," Elis recalled. "I'd watch as they carried things into their hole and greeted each other. I used a magnifying glass, and I realized that every big thing is composed of little things. Well, I love small things."

Peering through Elis' magnifying glass, I inspected his minute drawings of daily life on the ABC's. He had found beauty in the miniature scale and its intimacy. Appropriately, I thought, for the small, sociable islands he calls home.

Winter swimmers find peace at Curaçao's Knip Bay. Nearby in 1795, some 1,500 salt-plantation slaves rebelled and marched on Willemstad. Dutch troops finally suppressed this uprising, and put its three leaders to death after public torture.

3 | Barbados

Written by Mary Ann Harrell and photographed by Donald J. Crump

Cane fields still cover the gentle terrain of Barbados, long a single-crop "sugar colony."
At Andrew's Factory (above) in the parish of St. Joseph, men lop the stems and trim the
leafy tops that women gather for use as cattle feed, while tractors speed the cane to the
mill. Today tourism and manufacturing bring a new prosperity to the island, now a nation;
but, as one of its artists says, "The cane takes the best land."   65

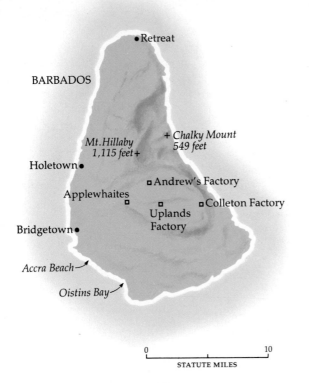

BARBADOS

- Retreat
- + Chalky Mount 549 feet
- Mt.Hillaby 1,115 feet +
- Holetown •
- Applewhaites □
- Andrew's Factory □
- Colleton Factory □
- Uplands Factory □
- Bridgetown •
- Accra Beach
- Oistins Bay

0   10

STATUTE MILES

Easternmost of the Antilles, Barbados ranks as a small island by size but an MDC—more developed country—by success. One of the most densely populated places on earth, it holds some 250,000 people on 166 square miles. Its shape inspires comparison to a ham, a leg of mutton, or a pear-shaped emerald. Its easterly position gave it safety in the days of sail because hostile warships from other islands faced an awkward beat against the trade winds to reach it. It remained a British colony, with a stubborn legislature of its own after 1639, until 1966. In that year it became an independent monarchy —like Canada or Australia—within the Commonwealth.

"I'll tell you: God made the world. Then He said, 'I must have somewhere for Myself—a place to rest.' So He made Barbados."

From the vantage of 87 years, Mr. John Bright Deane was explaining his homeland, easternmost of the Antilles. For me, he sums up much of its human flavor with his Bible-tinged eloquence, his readiness to welcome a visitor, and the humor that seasons his unabashed pride in the island. The setting evoked the central fact of its history. We stood in the shadow of a plantation house, with a donkey braying as it tugged a cart up the hillside, the trade wind rippling the fields of cane that surrounded us.

Sugar has dominated life in Barbados since the 1640's. It meant fortunes for a few, the white planters who built up large estates. It meant loss for the less fortunate whites who left for other lands or sank into poverty. It imposed suffering on the black slaves who worked the crops, plotted doomed rebellions, died worn out. Even after slavery was legally abolished in 1834, the rule of the prosperous white "plantocracy" continued almost unshaken for a century, while the lot of the workers remained virtually unchanged.

Out of this grim history, the people of Barbados have shaped the strength I observed in the Deanes. Mrs. Deane, in her late 70's, manages a sugar estate. She left a business discussion to ask graciously how I liked Barbados.

A lot. Like thousands of visitors since World War II—more than 300,000 in 1978 alone—I've found it a superlative place to rest. I sampled its attractions on a cruise stop a decade ago: swimming and sunbathing on a white-sand beach; lunching on fresh-caught flying fish; sauntering through Bridgetown, watching the schooners load and unload at the Careenage; sight-seeing on a country drive. I never forgot the way a taxi driver went in one breath from an earthy yell at another driver to "How do you like Barbados, mistress?"

In 1979 I found something even more appealing than beaches, and I'm a beach devotee. I was in the midst of a success story. Since November 30, 1966, Barbados has been an independent nation within the Commonwealth, gaining a reputation for stability and progress, and the fun of a holiday weekend in winter suggested some of the reasons.

"This the land, our island land. . . . our only land. . . . where Africa and Britain meet in exile. . . ." Even the small children around me listened as members of the public library staff read tributes to island life in poetry and prose, standard English and broad Bajan dialect. Sunlight and cloud shadow raced over the outdoor stage; a little boy nibbled fried fish as he heard "The Making of the Drum," and a stylish little girl sipped a Pepsi during a story about the early days of the Redlegs, the poor whites of Barbados.

Since 1977 the Holetown Festival has commemorated the landing of the first English settlers and the first slaves near a cove on the Caribbean coast on February 17, 1627. ("There's a dispute about the date," I was told, "but we're using this one.") If that first party came divided in most respects, the program stressed that they were equals in "homesickness for the Africa and the England they had left behind." This careful awareness of shared humanity marks life in Barbados today.

Until recently, only the English tradition claimed public honor and space in schoolbooks. Barbados still acknowledges its importance. Early on the morning of February 16, broadcaster Alfred Pragnell took me and my photographer-colleague Don Crump north and inland to a country church for a wreath-laying ceremony at the grave of William Arnold, remembered as "first ashore" of the new settlers. His descendant William Arnold Armstrong—a sturdy John Bull figure—placed flowers; historian Edward Stoute told of family details; the Reverend C.V.S. Belle read Scripture with Anglican dignity; and schoolchil-dren in crisp uniforms sang "O God, Our Help in Ages Past."

"We never studied our own history like this when I was a boy," the Honourable Burton Hinds told me afterward. A man of the new democracy, he had come to lay the official wreath as Member of Parliament for the parish and Speaker of the House of Assembly. "We learned all about the Norman Conquest—and nothing about, say, Saba or Statia."

Other aspects of the festival kept the decorum of the Empire. Ladies of the parish filled the Church of St. James with gladiolus, ginger lilies, anthuriums, ferns; the church displayed its antique silver, such as a chalice "Devoted *by* yᵉ Honble Coˡˡ John Standfast." On Sunday morning Their Excellencies the Governor-General and Lady Ward arrived for worship in a gleaming white Daimler; in official and social life they represent the Crown, for Barbados is still a monarchy.

Military pomp marked a Friday night tattoo under floodlights at a nearby playing field. The band of the Royal Barbados Police Force played marches; the Mounted Troop swirled through their musical ride, with torches blazing on their lances. This won murmurs of praise: "It nice—it really nice." And visiting sailors from H.M.S. *Scylla* joined a parade through the town, with children rushing at their heels.

But the dominant mood was Bajan: informal, at once easygoing and energetic, self-controlled and good-humored.

"Only the food and the music are really 'authentic,'" Alfred had warned me. The so-called "tuk band"—wiry men of middle age or better, with flute, kettledrums, and an iron triangle—performed all day Saturday, weaving through an ever-thickening crowd. Before them pranced a man wearing a garish red-and-yellow mask and a print dress, whisking up the skirt to taunt the musicians with a glimpse of black lace.

"Nobody's   *(Continued on page 72)*   67

*F*ighting *for quality and profit, manager Geoffrey Cox of Applewhaites plantation helps battle a cane fire. Burned cane, easier to cut than green, gives poorer syrup unless harvested immediately; producers in Barbados wage yearly campaigns against the fire menace. In the terminal at Bridgetown's Deep Water Harbour, a front-end loader moves sugar at a ten-story mountain awaiting shipment. Rum for export (left) enjoys a high reputation; but sugar enters a glutted market throughout the world. Barbadians hope to find alternative uses for their principal crop. New processing machinery that separates the rind from the juicy pith of the cane offers promise: Dr. Caspar Warnaars, of Canada's aid program, displays samples of sturdy panelboard made from the rind.*

*Celebrations called Crop-
over, beginning in
June, mark the end of the
cane harvest. At right, Lady
Ward, wife of the Governor-
General, holds a parasol over
the Queen of the 1979
festival: Mrs. Ianthe Herbert
earned her title by loading
513 tons of cane during the
season. Above, Bajan men
attend the effigy of "Mr.
Harding," burned on the
final night. He may
symbolize the cruel bosses of
post-slavery days. At left, in
a contest for decorated
donkey carts, pupils of
St. Gabriel's School ride in
a prizewinning entry; 1979
as International Year of the
Child supplied its theme.*

sure if that owes more to English folk tradition or to African dances," said Alfred. Such antics shocked the genteel writers of the past into silence; as poet Edward Kamau Brathwaite has said, the true popular life of Barbados runs underground—like the rivers.

On Saturday morning the Mighty Gabby, the reigning calypso king, had performed, first shouting to a tourist group, "Make sure you get out of the bus and come to we festival too." The crowd gave him a big hand for his song "Take Down Nelson!" Barbados has bragged for decades of its monument to the great naval hero; Lord Nelson's statue still complicates traffic at Bridgetown's waterfront. But Gabby's song demands, "Take down Nelson, take down Nelson—put up a Bajan man!"

Gabby saved for last a song that people kept calling for: "Pelé!" He spelled out its importance for any puzzled tourist: "Here in Barbados, we believe in justice. We believe in peace. We believe in harmony. We believe in *respect for the law!*" Pelé—nickname of a popular Bajan athlete, Victor Parris—had been shot, fatally, in May 1978. The case was still unsolved, and horrifying rumors hinted at a cover-up. Gabby's voice rang out—*"Who kill Pelé?"*—and applause broke like a storm wave.

That flair of drama aside, the day eased along, with buggy rides for grown-ups and pony rides for children, and all the attractions of a street fair. I met a sturdy feminist selling T-shirts that said "SUPPORT WOMEN NOW." A national commission has suggested legal reforms to assure equal justice for women, who are already gaining new status and career opportunities.

I also met Fielding Babb, tugboat officer and artist, and bought one of his forthright oils. It conveys the endurance of a little hillside house: gray coral foundation, gray weathered wood, galvanized roof, louvered shutters open to the faithful wind.

I sampled fish an' floats, salt cod and sweetish deep-fried dough. I tried fresh cane juice (exceedingly sweet), homemade ginger beer (very gingery), and a drink called maubey made from the bark of a tree (pleasantly bittersweet). I ate homemade sugar cakes and coconut bread and home-parched peanuts. An ad for Home Farm Fruit Drinks summed it up: "Gulpalicious and Swallowrific!"

Sunday, after church, brought family-outing crowds to the beach for a fish fry and water-sports gala; and everybody just relaxed, even some of the sun-reddened visitors who had seemed a bit self-conscious on Saturday. "You see it in their faces," Gabby told me later; "but as soon as they know someone, you can see them relax." I saw it—and felt it—myself.

One blond Barbadian native had warned me, "We don't say 'white' and 'black' the way you do. If we must make a distinction, we say 'fair' or 'dark.'" Then I met another, in Bridgetown, who said lightly, "I have about twenty first cousins and twice as many second cousins—of all colors. We see one another according to congeniality, not color."

To some extent geography has affected these matters, as Senator John Wickham told me. Son of a crusading editor who fought for political rights for the majority, he edits the literary magazine *Bim* and a new magazine for children. "You start with an island. A *small* island, 166 square miles. A small *British* island, no other domination. And, always, two races. Size and terrain. Here, the slaves had no mountains, no inland to escape to. Therefore a greater hazard of rebellion; and therefore stronger repression—drum music used to be forbidden, you know. But I think Barbados has been saved by its limited resources and its history—they've taught us that we cannot dissipate our energies."

What distinguishes Barbados?

"Here life is rather staid; less exciting than on other Caribbean islands,

72

maybe. We are providing hot lunches for all schoolchildren, but we don't call that socialism."

He hinted, delicately, that past distinctions of color are not dead. "Socially, some constraints remain." But all citizens give their nation "a fierce, intense, very vocal loyalty."

The Honourable H. A. Vaughan, a former judge and diplomat, concurred: "Bajans of all sorts, breeds, origins, and conditions have a great pride in Barbados." He stressed two points. Barbados has always had its own elected legislature, and "outsiders said the same things about it in the past that they say today. 'Aloof and self-satisfied.' 'Conceited; regarding themselves as perfect.' 'A very *respectable* island.' " He spoke of a way of life that seeks to assure goodwill by good manners—and he smiled. "We may be much too inclined to think highly of ourselves."

Bajan manners are consistently excellent; in government offices and posh suburban gardens; in noisy sugar mills and tranquil country lanes. Visitors talking of the attractions of the island repeatedly say, "the people." A lady in public life told me of a troubled moment on a television talk show in New York: "I was trying to convey the courtesy of Barbadians, and I realized that it sounded like the 'simple friendly islander' cliché." Omowale Stewart, of DEPAM—De People's Art Movement—has asked bluntly if Bajans want to appear as the stereotype of the "smiling nigger." His own portraits answer that: Don Crump and I brought home, and prize, prints of his powerful study of a strong young father holding an infant. I met other artists who capture the dignity and the comedy of Bajan life, such as Karl Broodhagen and Timothy Callender, and found them generous guides to its customs and quirks—for instance, the way men sing hymns, in close harmony, after several rounds in a rum shop.

"People look out for you here," a Guyanese playwright told me. "Every-one's a potential traffic officer. Even a child will flag down traffic to let a car pull out of a blind entrance—and the traffic always stops. I've not seen that anywhere else in the Caribbean." A Jamaican economist added, "I used to think Barbados should have many more road signs. Now I think it would be a mistake. You can always ask somebody for directions, and you always get them. It keeps a human contact alive—a sense of community."

The sense of responsibility, on a face-to-face scale, tempers a spirited running battle in a two-party political system. Responsibility shows in a vigorous free press, full of letters-to-the-editor on countless public issues. All this contributes to the political stability that has helped to make Barbados the "Switzerland of the Caribbean," a center for international organizations.

At one extreme, Ken Corsbie runs T.I.E., an information center for theater people in the Caribbean, out of his small apartment in Christ Church. At another, the Caribbean Development Bank, with two sleek new office blocks overlooking the cane fields, tries to balance funds—and political considerations—for the good of a needy region.

CADEC, the development agency for the Caribbean Conference of Churches, grapples with economic and social issues. At its Barbados center I met the Reverend Andrew Hatch, Anglican priest, activist, and Senator. (The Governor-General of Barbados appoints 12 Senators chosen by the Prime Minister, 2 chosen by the Opposition, and 7 at his own discretion.) "It's not that the Church is political," said my host briskly, "but to help people it must work in politically sensitive areas." A slight, brown-haired man, at once harried and serene, he listed concerns ranging from solar energy to city planning. The conversation reached the riddle of Barbados today: how a society marked by generations of injustice has achieved so much, so peacefully. His (Continued on page 85) 73

74

Plumy casuarina trees and plots of growing cane mark ridges and slopes in the hilly northeast near Chalky Mount, where clay deposits have sustained a pottery tradition for more than a century. A craft comparatively new to Barbados, batik-making, finds many customers among tourists. Veronica Cox dyes a length of fabric for a studio at Colleton Factory, an old sugar plantation. Near Retreat, in St. Lucy, a small villager completes her call at one of the many public telephones sited throughout the island. Her generation may grow up taking such well-maintained, fast-expanding public amenities and utilities for granted. Her elders, like the dignified woman at left, remember the decades of hardship and watch each step of national progress with pride.

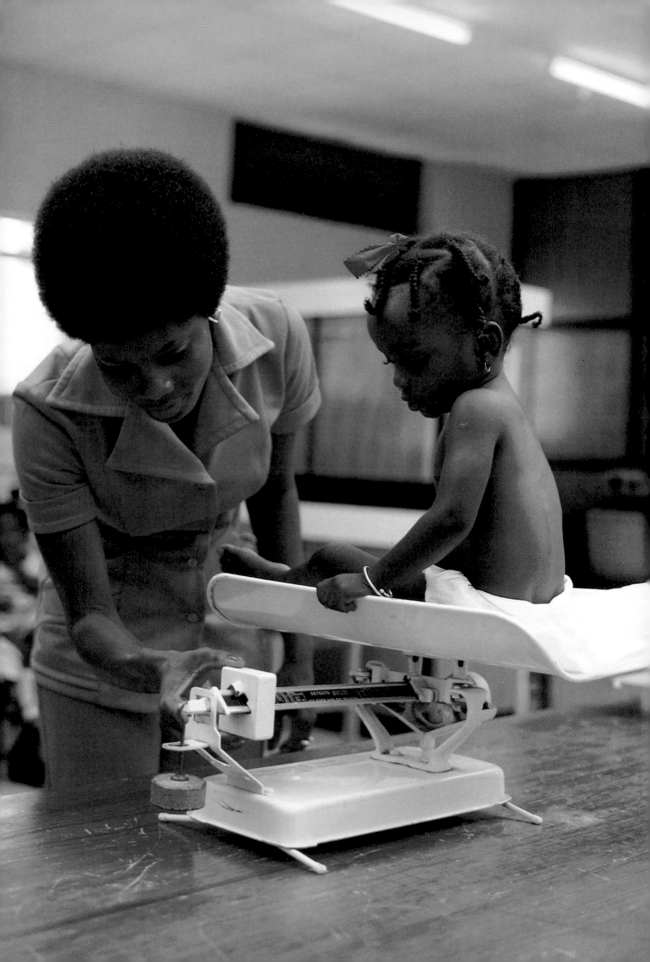

As Governor-General, Sir Deighton Ward represents Her Majesty. At the hospital named in honor of Elizabeth II, an aide in the Nutrition Centre weighs a winsome two-year-old—part of a public health program that has almost ended death from deficiency diseases of childhood in Barbados. Below, head teacher Osbert Vaughan of St. Saviour's Mixed (or coed) School advises a boy in Class Four. Barbadians value education as all-important.

Swimmers take an evening dip at historic Oistins Bay, a center for fishermen on the

southern coast; by sundown the small boats, their work done, ride at their moorings.   79

*B*uffet "planter's style" echoes the lavish hospitality of old for guests at the Hilton. Delicacies for Sunday lunch often include roast suckling pig. Below, a Bajan bandsman joins a conga line of Americans and Europeans at the Rockley Resort Hotel and Beach Club; a young couple plays in the surf on Accra Beach; with his cutlass a coconut vendor opens a shell for customers during the Holetown Festival in February.

tlantic breakers swirl their treacherous currents along the rocky eastern shore. Inland, in St. Philip, Mrs. Leotta Jones tends her yard with her young friend Deana Peters for company. Her home of 40 years exemplifies the cherished chattel houses of Barbados. At the heart of Bridgetown, an obelisk honors the dead of World Wars I and II. Beyond it, Lord Nelson's statue still stands in Trafalgar Square amid busy crosswalks; to his left lies the old Careenage, long a shelter for small craft and interisland ships.

*C*ricket, amateur or pro, ranks as the national sport. Here West Indies and Australia compete in a one-day professional match. With good follow-through, Joel Garner bowls a fast one to an Aussie batsman; a tea break refreshes everyone. Final score: West Indies 159 runs, Australia 201.

voice softened: "It's only God's mercy, and the good nature of the Bajans. . . ."

Good nature, and good government, face continual tests in an economy dependent on imports. "We import your inflation," a diplomat told me bluntly. Barbados imports bottled gas for cooking, cataract needles for eye surgery, license tags for dogs, much of its food. Luxury items for the tourist are bargains. Few necessities are. "This is a prosperous island," a manufacturer told me, "but most people work for $70 Bajan a week: about $35 U. S."

At the Barbados Workers' Union Labour College, I met union leader Evelyn Greaves, M.P. for St. Lucy, who had minimum pay scales at hand. Shop assistants, $84 Bajan per week. Hotel workers, $73. Truck drivers, $2.88 per hour.

Rates for harvesting sugar are by the ton. Burned cane, easier to handle but poorer in quality, means slightly lower pay. Cutting and cleaning, the meanest job for the strongest men in the hot sun, brings $5.29 per ton burned, $5.75 green. A cutter may clear 25 tons per week. Often, women do the loading—for $5.25 per ton (burned) or $5.75 (green). Mr. Greaves' pleasant voice suddenly turned low and intense: *That's the work our parents did, to educate us.*

Education in Barbados is supremely important, even sacred. Literacy is almost universal. School policy stirs hot debate. Everyone sees education as one key to a better future; and decades of poverty have left Bajans with a Puritanical fervor for good work, thrift, and something to show for it.

"You want to know about life in Barbados? Ask me, man; I get around, I really get around!" Ricardo Clarke, in his early 20's, has held two full-time jobs at once. He belongs to two sports clubs, a political group, and his church's parish youth group. "I was rich in my mind, but I couldn't take advanced exams because my mother couldn't pay. I don't plan to marry until I can make my mother com-

fortable—then I can be comfortable too."

Ken S. Barrow, local general manager for an electronics firm, worries about jobs for young men like this. Manufacturing is the fastest-growing sector of the economy. From a work force of 110,000 it employs 15,000 in scores of factories. "I don't think IDC—the Industrial Development Corporation—can build buildings fast enough!" But, he says, new jobs are mostly in light industry and often go to young women. Unemployment stands at 15 percent; tourism and sugar offer primarily seasonal work.

Government takes a major role in economic matters. The Prime Minister, the Right Honourable J.M.G.M. Adams—nicknamed Tom—is also Minister of Finance and Planning. He told me of policy on inflation and prices—"Yes, we have price control here"—and progress in social services. "We're building clinics all over the island, and housing—that's the last area where we still rank as a developing country."

Business is the last realm where the old "white establishment" still rules. I saw a Bajan way of dealing with this delicate matter in seminars at Yoruba Yard, a center for a new, and controversial, attention to an African heritage. University professors, bankers, lawyers, accountants, and businessmen—some white—met for panel discussions marked by formal courtesy, intellectual weight, jokes, and hard-hitting exchange. The theme: "Is there a future for black business in Barbados?" The audience, almost all black, commented freely. Good points were acknowledged: "Hear hear!" "For true!" "Amen!" and "Right on!" I heard a gray-haired man say, "This head of mine has carried loads all over this island for sixpence an evening. What can the small man do in this country?" Just once I heard measured rage in a question from the floor: Why were whites invited to speak here?

Yoruba's leader, Elton Mottley, a vivid man with a moderate Afro, jumped lithely onto the stage. "First," his voice was sardonic, "I believe that every dog should have his day. And," his voice was somber, "without including them I see no hope at all."

Silence.

The questioner nodded. "Fair enough," he said. The debate went smoothly on.

That exchange, to me, sums up the strength of Barbados: a profound sense of "fair enough" governing the most bitter as well as the most agreeable aspects of life.

As Gabby told me, "I think we should certainly keep our statue of Nelson—I just think it belongs in the museum!" And I remember the comment of a living hero, the great cricketer Sir Garfield Sobers, once compared by an Aussie star to a "golden eagle among scraggy sparrows." ("Nobody," Ricardo Clarke told me, "ever came onto the field with his mixture of aggression and grace!")

I had heard from an eyewitness how the Queen knighted Gary Sobers on the Garrison Savannah in 1975: "There were people up in trees, people everywhere—you couldn't have run a needle between them. And when Her Majesty said, 'Rise, Sir Garfield,' a sound went up that I never heard before or since. It was as if your whole island were being knighted before your eyes!"

It was Sir Garfield who said, when I mentioned Barbados' popularity and good repute, "You can't really learn from praise. You only learn when people criticize you."

I want to go back. There are so many people I want to see again, to catch up on family news and public affairs. To see new paintings and hear new calypsos and find out how a new novel is coming along. To revisit Villa Nova or other stately homes, like Mullins Mill, that may be open under the auspices of the National Trust. To notice the intricate trim of the little wooden houses with names like Ebenezer and Perseverance. To see the new houses built with "lumber" made from sugarcane rind, thanks to the new equipment I saw being tested at Uplands Factory.

To hear the whistling frogs shrill in a garden at dusk. To see the salt haze turn the afternoon golden over the hills in the Scotland district. To drive through the country at night when the cane ripples under a foamy-white full moon. To stroll along Baxters Road in the evening through a Bajan crowd and hear jukebox disco or the Gospel Comforters, and get fresh fish cooked over live coals.

I might even get back to a beach.

Late one afternoon after the first ceremonies of Crop-over—the end of the cane harvest—I had a fragment of time for a swim. Then, just as I was settling down to wait for sunset, a dozen men and women came onto the beach, all but two or three in religious garb. "They're Spiritual Baptists," a beachwear vendor told me; "I haven't seen them here before." They prepared a center of worship on the sand as people came up to watch. A man announced with great dignity that some might scoff, but they thought it right to bear witness to their faith among their visitors. Nobody scoffed. We heard Scripture, and prayer; High Anglican litany, and speaking in tongues. We sang such hymns as "Sweet Hour of Prayer" in what a young spectator quietly described as "rum-shop harmonies." We sang "Let the lower lights be burning, send a gleam across the wave. . . ." And the sun slipped down into the Caribbean, sparkles of brightness glimmered from the yachts at their moorings, and it was finally time to rest.

Bajans and summer tourists watch respectfully as a member of a small Spiritual Baptist group, candle in hand, leads an unusual service of witness on the beach near the Yacht Club. White cloth covers bowls of rice and other food, later cast by women into the quiet sea.

4 | **Along the Windwards**

Written by Charles McCarry and photographed by Cotton Coulson

Sails sweep the harbor of St. George's, Grenada, during a regatta on Easter Sunday. The reliable northeast trades that send yachts along the Windwards today gave these islands their English name—and shaped a colonial past reflected in multi-hued buildings of French and English architectural styles. Smallest and southernmost of the new Windward nations, Grenada in 1974 became the first to gain independence from Great Britain.

89

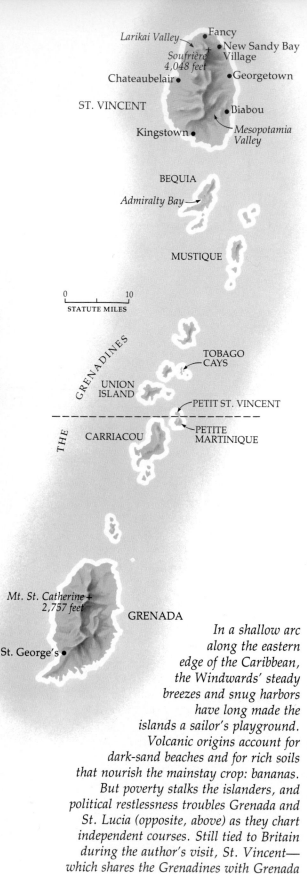

ST. VINCENT

Larikai Valley
Fancy
New Sandy Bay
Village
Soufrière
4,048 feet
Chateaubelair
Georgetown

Biabou

Kingstown
Mesopotamia
Valley

BEQUIA

Admiralty Bay

MUSTIQUE

0   10
STATUTE MILES

GRENADINES

TOBAGO
CAYS

UNION
ISLAND

PETIT ST. VINCENT

PETITE
MARTINIQUE

THE

CARRIACOU

Mt. St. Catherine
2,757 feet

GRENADA

St. George's

*In a shallow arc
along the eastern
edge of the Caribbean,
the Windwards' steady
breezes and snug harbors
have long made the
islands a sailor's playground.
Volcanic origins account for
dark-sand beaches and for rich soils
that nourish the mainstay crop: bananas.
But poverty stalks the islanders, and
political restlessness troubles Grenada and
St. Lucia (opposite, above) as they chart
independent courses. Still tied to Britain
during the author's visit, St. Vincent—
which shares the Grenadines with Grenada
—celebrated nationhood in October 1979.*

90

I had met *Sirocco* only the day before, but I was already a little in love with her. She was a great beauty; her 75-foot hull was as white as a bridal veil, her hatches gleamed with varnish, her brightwork caught mirror images of her billowing sails. In her youth she had sailed in famous blue-water races and now, beating into the trade winds, she quivered with eager spirit.

It was a perfect June morning, and *Sirocco,* her starboard gunwale awash in a six-foot granite-gray sea, was in the open Atlantic between World's End Reef and Palm Island in the Grenadines. These islands—hundreds of them, a few inhabited—stretch from Grenada, the most southerly of the Windwards, to its nearest "big" neighbor, St. Vincent. They are the breakwater between the surly Atlantic and the limpid Caribbean; five miles westward we would have been in another sea. *Sirocco* was happy enough where she was, and so were we. The tropic sun glittered like a doubloon, and this was the first day of our voyage through some of the loveliest waters on the planet. *Sirocco* cut through the waves like a sculptor's chisel, driven home by the hammer of the trades.

Her captain, a Minnesota Norseman named Jim Steivang, held the helm with one hand and a breakfast sandwich with the other—ham and eggs would have blown off the plate. The canvas strummed. "This is *mild* compared to what we'll encounter up-island," Jim bellowed cheerfully. "But all we have to do is set our sails—the trades will take us to St. Martin without a single tack."

Here "up-island" is north and "down-island" is south. We were sailing down-island, on a brief detour. On our starboard beam, the twin-needle peaks of Union Island snagged a passing cloud. Ahead, their colors muted by distance, lay Petit St. Vincent and Petite Martinique and, looming beyond them, the smoky-blue heights of Carriacou.

Carriacou, with Petite Martinique and the mother island of Grenada, is one of the three main islands that make up Grenada, smallest nation in the Western Hemisphere. Long known as the "Isle of Spice," Grenada has welcomed travelers with the fragrance of nutmeg and mace, clove and cinnamon. But on March 13, 1979, it had a whiff of gunpowder. A small group of armed rebels, striking before dawn, overthrew the elected, but notoriously corrupt and repressive, government of Sir Eric Gairy, Prime Minister since 1974.

Not long after the coup, I arrived in Grenada by air, and found soldiers of the People's Revolutionary Government lining the roof of the terminal. They were very young, but stern, nervously fingering automatic weapons. Their leaders feared that Sir Eric, who had been at the United Nations on March 13, might try to invade Grenada with mercenary troops.

Within a mile of the airport a hospitable Grenadian, as young as the soldiers, hailed my taxi. "Hey man, you ever smell nutmeg?" he asked me. He led me over to a tree, picked the fruit, peeled it to show me the red petticoat of mace, and held the kernel of nutmeg to my nostrils. He rode on with me into St. George's, the capital, stopping us to pluck a mango or a lime or a banana for me from roadside trees. By the time we reached the city with its pastel houses bright against the volcanic mountainside, I held in my lap all the ripened fruits of this breezy Eden.

Forty miles north, all was calm when *Sirocco* dropped anchor off Petite Martinique. Photographer Jodi Cobb spotted a schooner abuilding on the beach; we chugged ashore by dinghy, taking cold beer to share with the three shipwrights working under a cassia tree.

A compact chap named Macaulay John De Roche was swinging an adze; its handle was a twisted branch with the bark still on it, but the blade was razor-sharp. He was steadying a log with his bare foot, missing his toes by fractions of an inch as he shaped a

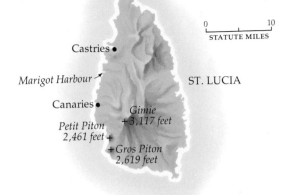

perfect four-by-four timber. Behind him stood the skeleton of the schooner—keel of greenheart, ribs of mangrove.

He held up a length of whittled plywood with ship's framing in miniature glued to it. Looking through it at the actual vessel I saw the two—scale model and ship—as one. "That," he laughed, "is a Petite Martinique blueprint!"

Macaulay has been building boats since he was five years old, and his father was his first teacher. You would see his father's world if you could hold the island up to your eye—the single dirt road tamped smooth by bare feet, the goats tethered in dooryards, the trees laden with breadfruit and mango and papaya, the patches of yam and cassava, the little heap of snapper and hind and grunt on the pier, the sailmakers working to a song under the open sky, children's voices pealing like bells.

"We eat what grows, make everything we can, and smuggle what we can't make; it has always been so," a cheery schooner captain told me.

It may not be so much longer. The Windwards were astir with change.

The reasons are plain. "From the deck of a yacht, these islands are paradise," said a young secretary to Maurice Bishop, the leader of Grenada's revolution. "But for the people, this is the Third World." Resentments run deep. On Union Island, my 15-year-old son John, already stunned by his first real glimpse of poverty, was shocked by an exchange with a lad in rags: "You American?" John *(Continued on page 96)*

*N*ature flaunts its brilliance in Grenada, where abundant rain—more than 150 inches annually in some areas—fosters an agrarian, cash-poor economy. Schoolchildren wait out a shower in a "parlour," a convenience store village style; banana harvesters shelter under plastic sacking used to protect the island's "green gold." Nutmeg by the basketful brought Grenada fame as the West's "Isle of Spice"; the valuable mantle, mace, echoes the red of flamboyant blossoms at an islander's home in the countryside.

*"*A *region of enchanted reefs . . . suggestive of the glory of creation." So author Charles*

McCarry found the Tobago Cays, a queen among anchorages in the Caribbean.

nodded proudly. "We work hard," said the lad bitterly, "so you can be rich."

Few in these islands are rich, even by their own standards. Macaulay John De Roche, the most skilled of workers, takes six months to build a schooner, earning perhaps $19 U. S. a day. Fishermen work on a cooperative basis. Six men might stay out for a week on a 30-foot decked sloop and sell their catch for $700 U. S. On that they must maintain the boat—and six families. On the sugar islands, a man might get $1.95 for each ton of cane cut under a staring sun.

This sort of work touches a nerve as raw as a whipped back. A few students escape into universities. But an island with 100,000 residents—how many doctors and lawyers, how many poets, even, does it need? Grenada has 133 square miles, about twice the area of the District of Columbia, with some 110,000 people at home and perhaps as many more working abroad; nearly half the "home" work force is unemployed.

Wherever I went, talking with a Prime Minister or a jobless Ph.D. or a boat boy, I heard of the same dilemma: Go away from the only place you love, or change the way that place is ruled. Sometimes in strident anger, sometimes in whispers, they vowed that they would have justice—enough jobs, enough protein in their diet, enough schools. A graffito I saw on a peeling wall up-island runs through my head yet: *Stamp out corruption! Prevent an eruption!*

Our boat lived in the one unchangeable element. The summer trades blow out of the south and east, and we sailed north before them to a region of enchanted reefs. Our landfall was the Tobago Cays. Here, only inches below the surface or fifteen feet down, we swam in snorkel gear through a realm of living things so elaborate, so many-hued, so suggestive of the glory of creation, that it seemed the Creator lingered there still. We stayed for hours, enthralled, in this crystalline water.

That afternoon, we applied sunburn remedies to one another's backs. All of us were as red as the delicate shells of the conch that our cook, Marion Herzog, turned into delicious canapés.

The temptation to linger was very strong. But the rest of the Grenadines lay ahead, and beyond them St. Vincent and St. Lucia. *Sirocco,* at only six or seven knots, could make easily twenty miles or so before the sudden sunset of these latitudes, so we paused for a night at Mustique, a hideaway isle for the jet set. Some of us dined in Basil's Bar, a yachtsmen's haunt. In mid-meal the lights went out. "The electricity she tired, got to rest," explained the amiable waiter, who sang for us in a lilting tenor.

Next day we spied ahead of us the hills of Bequia, a whaler's island for nearly two centuries. In 1979 two humpbacks, a mother and her calf, swam into the harbor, and most of the 7,000 Bequians lined the beach to watch. Then the whalers pursued them to Mustique, killed them, and towed them to uninhabited Petit Nevis for butchering. Athneal Ollivierre, for fifty years Bequia's most skilled harpoonist, told me about it: "No whales came for many months, so it was a blessing when two came to us. They gave five thousand pounds of meat, and the feast, it lasted for days!"

Inland, I saw women in bright cottons, surrounded by a nimbus of laughter, swinging the hoe on steep hillsides planted with cassava, peas, and young corn. "The women tell us when to plant," said Bill Adams, my Bequian companion. "They know about the moon and the soil."

We had to wait out nearly a week of rain at Bequia before the sun came out to dry our laundry. A pleasant 24-year-old American lass, Kathy Sass, warned me against swimming in Admiralty Bay. "Staphylococcus—the harbor is full of it." Waste dumped from yachts has bred this pollution in many anchorages up- and down-island.

Our laundry dry at last, we sailed

for St. Vincent. Haze obscured even Soufrière, the great volcano that had begun erupting violently on Good Friday, April 13. At last a landmark took form: "Ah," said Jim, "so *that's* where we are!" We anchored off the southern tip of the island.

In Kingstown, the capital, matchbox houses, with shops mixed in, lined the streets. A delightful crowd thronged the way—schoolchildren, all dressed in neat navy-blue uniforms, boys in striped ties and girls in snowy collars.

The eruption of Soufrière was still on everyone's lips. In the last great explosion, in 1902, 1,565 perished and thousands were left homeless. This time no one had died or been injured, though the Good Friday eruption was the first of twenty-odd. The largest sent millions of tons of dust more than 60,000 feet into the sky. Much of the island, 18 miles long and 11 wide, was coated with ash.

A young fellow who rowed me back to *Sirocco* took a philosophical view: "It gives the new generation their thing to remember, like the ancient people had 1902. When *I* am old and they say, 'When you saw that cloud and the ashes blew down and the stones hit the houses, were you scared?' I will reply, 'I was scared!'"

I heard from Durrant Liverpool, a government spokesman, how 22,000 people had been evacuated. Seismographs, linked by radio telemetry to a research unit in Trinidad, had picked up warning signs. People in roadless areas in the shadow of Soufrière were taken off in boats. The refugees were settled in camps in the south; two months later, 10,000 remained. "At the height of the crisis," Mr. Liverpool said, "it cost $30,000 U. S. a day to feed these unfortunate people. We've had generous aid from abroad—about $450,000 in cash already, plus a lot of food. But of course that only paid for 15 days of care."

St. Vincent received a profound economic aftershock just as I arrived: London had cabled that an entire shipload of bananas exported after the eruption had arrived spoiled. T. M. Findlay of the Banana Growers Association told me that ash had affected the fruit "in a way we do not understand yet. We don't know how much of the crop will be lost." It takes nearly a year to produce a mature banana, and it was conceivable that the entire crop on the stem would be ruined. Then five thousand growers, many of them small farmers, would be losing critical income for a year or more.

These facts rang in my memory as I started out next morning to explore the windward coast. We passed the airstrip where relief supplies had come in. "There are many interestings on our drive today," said the good-humored driver, Carleton "Trinny" Coombes. "This is your first interesting."

The coastal road mounted into the precipitous emerald countryside. We stopped at the La Croix banana-boxing plant in the fertile Mesopotamia Valley. Lorry loads of green bananas were being brought in. Alfred Jackson, the supervisor, told me that normally the plant serves five or six hundred farmers, shipping as many as 210 tons of fruit a week. "Now we ship about half as much, and we cannot tell if it will spoil. Farmers are paid a guaranteed price—roughly, six cents U. S. a pound—so families are losing about $13 a week from their meager cash income. How will they live if bananas stop growing?"

Offshore, wild surf crashed on the beach, but it wasn't the frothy azure sea *Sirocco* had been sailing in. This was a dirty gray for hundreds of yards out—ash. And ash was everywhere. In midafternoon we reached our goal, the famous plantation Orange Hill Estates, on the lower slopes of Soufrière. Bananas hung unharvested, their bright green dimmed by the dust as a healthy face is blurred by the pallor of illness. Rank upon rank of coconut trees slumped under the same dispiriting pall.

We set sail at five the next morning with heavy hearts; along the leeward

Caulked and painted, Adelaide B. *awaits launching on Petite Martinique as islanders wedge logs under her keel. Throughout the Grenadines, boatbuilding represents an art born of commercial need and a native supply of sturdy cedarwood for planking; the lovingly crafted sloops and schooners carry a lively trade in imported foodstuffs, as well as produce or cattle hoisted aboard at Carriacou. Improvising comes easy to a would-be surfer and his friends, raised among islands where livelihoods—and reputations—depend heavily on seafaring skills learned at an early age.*

99

In a workshop on Bequia, Elmore Laidlow shapes the ribs of a model boat. Adult model-makers use local gumwood for detail-perfect copies of yachts and Bequian whaleboats. Children fashion gaily rigged coconut-shell schooners for sale to visitors, and more elaborate versions for regattas of their own.

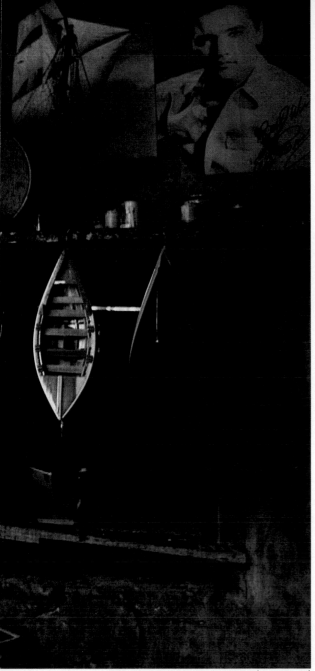

rain, and as *Sirocco* left land behind, she heeled and plunged in an ocean wind. Sheets of spray mingled with the downpour. We smashed onward through boisterous seas, and in late afternoon sighted the lofty headlands of St. Lucia, the famous Pitons.

We moored in a "hurricane hole" called Marigot Harbour, and next morning motored up to Castries, capital and hardworking port, loud with the shouts of stevedores and the clang of metal on metal. Castries, ravaged by fire twice in 30 years, has the grease-under-fingernails look of a raw new town.

Yet enchanted is the word for St. Lucia, a line of jagged mountains mantled with heavy rain forest; flamboyant trees, hibiscus, flocks of bright birds; lordly hogs and willful goats and strutting cocks roaming free. In one dooryard, I looked up through that misting rain that islanders call "liquid sunshine" and asked the man who lived there if he and his numerous family ate all the things that grew within hand's reach: breadfruit, mangoes, coconuts, limes, yams, sweet potatoes, cassava.

"You cannot stop us!" he cried with a laugh. I spoke in French, and he answered in Creole, the vernacular of St. Lucia and other islands once or currently held by France. Its vocabulary, based on French, contains English and a few Spanish words; its grammar echoes West African languages. Until a generation ago, St. Lucians spoke it as spontaneously as they breathed. Then they saw that English was the language of education and self-improvement, and ambitious parents would even beat their children for speaking anything else. Today Creole is making a comeback as the proud vocabulary of island identity.

A gifted young sculptor named Vincent Joseph Eudovic has married the idiom and materials of St. Lucia to techniques learned elsewhere. Eudovic, a bearded slender man, chatted with me in his workshop on a hilltop above Castries. Here, in (Continued on page 112)

coast, we saw little cause for optimism. From coastal plots to mountain forests, the land lay under a gray shroud. Two boys rowed out from the village of Chateaubelair. We asked about the crops. One of the boys grinned: "All mashup, man. Nothin' left."

Our last glimpse of St. Vincent, so lovely and so sad, was of Soufrière itself, the sun above it reddened by tons of dust that still hung in the atmosphere. We had been sailing in a flogging

*F*arm plots terrace the hills of St. Vincent in the fertile
Mesopotamia Valley (right). On the windward
coast, Atlantic rollers wash near-pristine beaches of
volcanic sand (PRECEDING PAGES). Intensive cultivation
gives this island its only exports. Below, a farmer
harvests rhizomes of arrowroot, an important item of
trade. Once sold exclusively as a food starch, it now coats
the surface of no-carbon copying paper. At the La Croix
boxing plant, a worker displays a fine hand of bananas.
His smile belies anxiety over most of the 1979 crop: A
volcanic eruption in April spewed ash that damaged the
fruit; an entire shipload spoiled; only at year's end did
production approach the normal—about 600 tons a week.

NATIONAL GEOGRAPHIC PHOTOGRAPHER JODI COBB (ABOVE)

105

eserted, the little northeastern village of New Sandy Bay stands beneath a pall of ash; just a few miles off, the volcano—the Soufrière—still rumbles. Short-range showers of rock, and far-flung ash, worked havoc with crops and sent 22,000 Vincentians fleeing to safety.

Clotted ash chokes the Larikai Valley on Soufrière's slopes shortly after the eruption of April 13. Mudflows clouded the water, altered river channels, and disrupted irrigation— yet another aspect of calamity.

Ash in the air at Georgetown forces a man to use a blanket as an emergency mask. Constant seismic monitoring helped avert fatalities; but at the Biabou Anglican Church (right) and dozens of other shelters, weary refugees—already among St. Vincent's poorest—drained the island's funds as Soufrière remained active for weeks. At left, a villager leaving home takes his livestock with him. Below, crammed with bundles of household possessions, the last dinghy casts off from Fancy, on the north coast.

NATHAN BENN (ABOVE, BELOW, AND OPPOSITE)

*W*ith emblems of nationhood held high, St. Lucians greet their independence on February 22, 1979. During a turbulent past, wars between France and Britain made this 238-square-mile island a prize that changed hands 14 times; since 1967, St. Lucia had governed itself as a state associated with Great Britain. At left, a jubilant Prime Minister John Compton displays the Constitution just presented by Her Majesty's representative, Princess Alexandra. Flags wave proudly at a schoolchildren's rally, their colors symbolizing cerulean sky and water, golden sunshine, black and white cultural influences. A high birth rate crowds the island; official unemployment estimates range about 15 percent, and St. Lucia's youth—roughly half the population age 14 or younger—faces an uncertain future.

Purveying cheap fuel for St. Lucia's stoves, Ira Moses tends her wares at the Castries charcoal market. The heavily wooded but mineral-poor island now looks toward the tapping of volcanic steam for relief from its crushing dependence on imported oil.

a compound of thatched huts, apprentices carve masks and figurines that sell to tourists—and give good value. Eudovic himself creates fantastical abstract shapes from woods he finds in the high rain forest.

"My favorite is laurier canelle, now very rare. I use only old roots, from trees cut down hundreds of years ago. In these roots I find the form of my art." He ran his hand over the satiny surface of a piece that seemed to move like a bird at his touch. Eudovic grew up in the forest, far from schools; when he was about eight, he began whittling toys with an old knife. "My mind told me there was more inside the wood," he explains. He went to Trinidad and then to Nigeria to study.

"I want to carve the world's best sculpture," he says. "I think I will. My art, in order to be whole, must be recognized first in the sight of the people."

Others were vying for recognition in the sight of St. Lucia's 118,000 people. Prime Minister John Compton, 15 years in power, headed the United Workers Party. The youthful, radical Labour Party called for bold new directions for St. Lucia, which had become an independent nation a few months earlier. Compton had tried to stimulate tourism, attract foreign investment, improve agriculture, extend education. His accomplishments, said the Labour Party, were signs of imperialism, only the privileged got privileges, and the benefits of development did not filter down.

Just a few days before the election I wandered through the island, hoping to catch a glimpse of the future. In Canaries, on the western coast, all sea-beaten lumber and fretwork balconies teetering over narrow streets, I caught a glimpse of the dexterous past. Women were doing their laundry in the river

that rushes through the town—rocks for scrub boards, sunlight for bleach. Beyond the stream, in the mist of a sudden rain, was a sight fit for a mythmaker: a young man riding bareback on a horse as dark and as splendidly alert as himself. They might have been a centaur, those two, with the sea before them and the mountains at their back, and the children of Canaries skipping along at their side.

Farther on, a government campaigner in a slouch hat sang a political speech in Creole; he danced to the rhythm of his argument, and his audience danced with him. Along the steep winding roads we saw many a truckload of hurrahing Labour supporters, most of them very young. They flew flags with the red star of their party, and scattered their handbills in tranquil villages. Children chased the speeding caravans, skipping to the rhythm of the sirens and the loudspeakers. One small joyous boy ran right out of his ragged short trousers, his only garment.

On election day, the Labour Party won with more than 25,000 votes out of 46,000—the votes of young people, analysts said, put the new regime in office.

Hearing this, I remembered a truckload of young men who stopped us on the road near St. Lucia's steaming old volcano. Their red-star flags waved against the verdant slope. They were screaming at me, and raising clenched fists. I wished to respond. But there is no universal gesture to tell someone from another world that you feel no anger, that you understand his, that you mean him no harm. So I merely stood where I was, an alien figure in a breathtaking landscape, with my arms at my sides, knowing that it was useless to smile. The young men drove away with their flags and their slogans into their future.

5 | The French Antilles

Written by Charles McCarry and photographed by Jodi Cobb

Rocher du Diamant—or H.M.S. Diamond Rock, *duly commissioned as a sloop-of-war in the Royal Navy—rides permanently at anchor less than two miles from bathers on Martinique's southwestern coast. In 1804, British sailors outfitted the rock with cannon to harass ships bound for French-held Martinique. But that island, with the exception of three brief periods of British occupation, has loyally flown the French flag since 1635.*

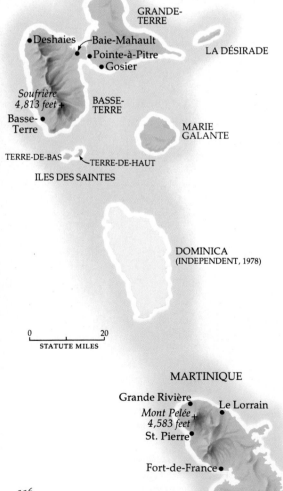

Grand Case●

Marigot●

(DUTCH) ●Philipsburg

ST. MARTIN

ST. BARTHÉLEMY
(ST. BARTS)

Gustavia●

0   10
STATUTE MILES

*Transatlantic départements of France,
Guadeloupe and Martinique both enjoy a
political status equal to that of Seine-et-
Marne, or any other counterpart on the
continent. Smaller islands such as St.
Barthélemy rank as dependencies
administered through Guadeloupe.
Citizens of all the French West Indies share
the legal rights of mainlanders, electing
deputies to the National Assembly in Paris.*

GUADELOUPE

GRANDE-
TERRE

●Deshaies —Baie-Mahault   LA DÉSIRADE
      ●Pointe-à-Pitre
      ●Gosier

Soufrière
4,813 feet+ BASSE-
      TERRE
Basse- ●
Terre   MARIE
          GALANTE

TERRE-DE-BAS   \TERRE-DE-HAUT

ILES DES SAINTES

DOMINICA
(INDEPENDENT, 1978)

0   20
STATUTE MILES

MARTINIQUE

Grande Rivière●
         ●Le Lorrain
Mont Pelée+
4,583 feet
St. Pierre●

Fort-de-France●

Diamond Rock—   ●Ste-Anne

Everywhere the French have gone as conquerors and civilizers, they have attempted to create a new France. Houses display the blue-and-white numbers seen on every French street; black policemen in *képis* stroll sidewalk cafés where people sip a *vin blanc cassis* while reading a local paper bright with the vermilion headlines of the provincial French press; the air is filled with the acrid smoke of *caporal* cigarettes and with the music of flattery.

Relaxing after a fine luncheon in the shade of an awning, on a balcony overlooking the harbor at Marigot in St. Martin, I mentioned this to a French acquaintance. He answered me with a Gallic shrug. "But you never quite succeed," I teased. "You've made your tropical islands *look* like France, but really they are only impersonations of her."

My friend lifted his eyes to the tattered Tricolor that flew from the crumbling ramparts of Fort Marigot, high above us. "*C'est vrai,*" he said. "True—but it is better to have a flawed portrait of one's beloved than none at all."

In the political sense, the French Antilles—Martinique; Guadeloupe with its offshore islets; St. Barthélemy and St. Martin (half of which is Dutch)—*are* France. They are overseas departments, governed from Paris, with exactly the same status as mainland counterparts. To their islands, the French have brought free universal education, the full benefits of a generous welfare system, and a noteworthy degree of prosperity and social justice.

Yet today even these islands are astir with talk of independence and with resentment of a history that began—whatever amends have since been made—in the enslavement of the islanders' African forebears.

"Martinique is in danger of death—economic, cultural, spiritual. The present system, which is a colonial system in disguise, cannot continue without causing the disappearance of Martinique," I was told in Fort-de-France.

"I want to make Martinique Martiniquan," the speaker continued. "She must find her soul. The evolution will be very rapid. Within ten years, she will be free."

But, I asked, would that not mean economic death—a frightening slide backward into squalor and malnutrition and illiteracy? The speaker smiled. "There are deaths and there are deaths," he said. "Some deaths can be very sweet, if they bring peace."

Was this some fiery young revolutionary? Far from it. I was seated in the simple office of Aimé Césaire, mayor of Fort-de-France, member of the French Chamber of Deputies, head of the *Parti progressiste martiniquais*—a man who looks like an angel in spectacles, speaks French like a member of the Académie Française, and who is one of the finest living poets of the French language.

Elsewhere, I heard similar analyses. In Guadeloupe, I was passing a pleasant hour with Roger Fortuné, a small landowner, civil servant, and historian, whose father was also a professional man. I asked him about a phrase I had been hearing over and over: "I *was* a black Frenchman." What about that past tense? He jabbed an emphatic forefinger into the tablecloth, making the wine goblets ring against one another.

"Me? French?" he cried. "It is an involuntary condition pure and simple. The French have been good 'royalty,' but in the French Revolution even the good royalty was swept away. It is the irresistible trend of history."

No one has proposed the means of living without the French. France showers billions of francs on these islands, buying their products at prices far above the world market.

In the department of Guadeloupe, which includes five dependencies with St. Martin and St. Barthélemy the most distant, there are 330,000 people living on 176,119 hectares (435,200 acres) of land. They own 96,000 automobiles. There are other gauges of wealth. For example, by law a housemaid must receive a minimum monthly wage equal to $166; her employer pays 33 percent of the wage into social security for her.

"People want to keep these advantages without a colonial administration," M. Fortuné told me. "They will have to work out a new way." But keeping the benefits while getting rid of the benefactors seems clearly impossible.

Off Guadeloupe lie the Iles des Saintes, islets of great natural beauty and marked social contrast. *Sirocco* dropped anchor in the harbor below the principal isle, Terre-de-Haut. With its mellow red roofs and whitewashed houses and the stone steeple of its church against the low green hillside, it looked as tidy and clean as any fishing port of northwest France. Norman and Breton sailors settled here in the 18th century, and the island's 1,700 souls are their descendants. Many are blond as Vikings; and cheeks of the tall men and their strapping wives are red as apples—but from rum, not Calvados.

Ninety percent of them bear one of the island's ten most common names. Thirty percent have the surnames of two prolific families, the Samson and the Cassin. A young physician, Patrick Chevailler, told me of the difficulties of making house calls: "I will ask, 'Where do you live?' and they will reply, 'In that white house there.' *All* houses here are white! I protest. '*Eh bien*, it's very simple to find—next door to Samson, just down the hill from Cassin!' "

This consanguinity has kept the community almost entirely white, though the old barriers seem to be lifting—one sees children of exotic beauty, having the blond hair and blue eyes of one parent and the café-au-lait skin of the other. For as long as Terre-de-Haut has been white, the other inhabited isle of the Saintes, Terre-de-Bas, has been wholly black.

Dr. Chevailler invited me to go with him to Terre-de-Bas, and included my 17-year-old son, (Continued on page 125)

orld of contrasts greets the visitor to Guadeloupe's main port and commercial center, Pointe-à-Pitre, where a window shopper may follow the current fashions and yet carry her produce to market in a decidedly traditional way. High-rise, low-rent apartments signal an end to corrugated shanties as the city strives to house its growing population of 25,000. Among the most developed islands in the Antilles, Martinique and Guadeloupe boast high literacy, good roads, and freedom

from the wracking poverty that plagues so much of the Caribbean. Their success stems primarily from infusions of financial aid from metropolitan France. Support prices for sugar and bananas also help their largely agricultural economy, which provides a living for nearly half the populace.

Comb and feathers clipped for combat, a fighting cock of
Guadeloupe will battle to the death unless its owner
intervenes. Pampered with madeira and the best corn money can buy,
the birds duel in crowded miniature arenas (above). Betting agents
shout out the odds, and spectators frantically place bets with hand
signals, at times staking hundreds of francs on a single match.

121

"**T**he work is hard, the pay bad," says cane grower Stephane Barlagne, at home with his wife, Francia, in Baie-Mahault on Guadeloupe. For thirty years they have raised sugarcane on rented land, using hoe and machete to plant, weed, and harvest. They spend grueling days in the tropic heat—only to find disappointment in the prices offered by cane buyers. One of their

11 children, Marthe, who works in Paris for the postal and telecommunications service, sent the miniature Eiffel Tower as "her first little gift"; their son Georges, a schoolboy just entering his teens, has not yet made definite plans for his future career.

Caleb, along on this leg of the voyage. Patrick hailed *Sirocco* early, and we fended off his flashy speedboat, *Bluebibou*, as it pitched and yawed in choppy waters. Tropical storm Claudette was bearing down on the islands and might become a hurricane; its leading edge of bruise-colored clouds was already boiling over the summit of a hill called le Chameau.

Bluebibou, we decided, could outrun the storm, and off we went at a speed that seemed dazzling, in a racket that seemed deafening after *Sirocco*'s ladylike ways. The doctor received many a friendly wave from fishermen. When dolphin fish are running, he said, a boat might take 500 or even 800 kilos that would sell on the pier for about $3 a kilo. Like all native Guadeloupians, the Saintois pay no taxes.

Terre-de-Bas consists of two villages, and it took Caleb and me less than an hour to tour the island in the back of a pickup truck. Here one sees poverty—ramshackle houses and people in rags. But we also noted a desalination plant for fresh water, and a power plant that supplies electricity to most homes. "They have TV sets—even color," Patrick told us later.

We passed a few hours in a bar: corrugated iron roof pitted with rust, a crumbling concrete floor, tables and benches made of scrap lumber. A scrawny hen wandered through, followed by three pullets that tried to eat the coins of sunlight that fell through the holes in the roof; and a goat looked in, shook its cynical black head, and turned away.

The Saintois whisper to strangers, but they shout to one another. The bar rang with their conversation. Though it was barely 9 a.m., fishermen were dropping in for a morning bracer. One man drank an entire liter of fiery white rum in less than twenty minutes; his friends broke his record repeatedly while I watched in wonder.

That evening, at dinner with a French sailmaker named Louis-Michel Le Doze, who has lived in Terre-de-Haut

Control by France for more than three centuries has left a distinctly Gallic imprint. "Everyone is Catholic," says a townsman of Deshaies, in northwestern Guadeloupe; "everyone goes to church." The devout come and go near la mairie, the town hall, as a post-office clock marks the hours. On Martinique, a small monument in the Atlantic coast town of Le Lorrain honors islanders who left the secure Caribbean to fight and give their lives for France in World War I.

125

for two years, I heard a superb account of small-island pride. "If I lived here for forty years," he said, "I would still be, in their phrase, *un sale blanc*—a dirty white." But, I protested, his neighbors themselves are white.

"They call all outsiders 'white,'" said Louis-Michel with a smile. "To them, Terre-de-Haut is the center of the universe. They believe they have the best boats, that they are the best fishermen, the best swimmers, the most beautiful people on earth.

"And then, of course, there are the *canadiennes.*"

"Now just who are they?"

"Women—no matter what nationality—who come here to have vacation love affairs with the locals. I have friends who do nothing for a living except make love. The girls buy them clothes, restaurant meals, and give them money. Naturally they believe they are the world's greatest lovers. Who wouldn't, if women traveled five thousand miles to be with them?"

To sail the six miles from Terre-de-Haut to Guadeloupe is to go from a music box into a foundry. Pointe-à-Pitre, the commercial center, fills the azure skies above it with the clangor of industry. Traffic storms the heights of Basse-Terre, the mountainous western wing of this butterfly island, with the élan of Napoleonic infantry. On Grande-Terre, the agricultural plain of the eastern wing, cane and other crops fall before the blades of the most modern farm machinery.

Lamenting all this progress, an acquaintance told me, "We have lost Africa!" A day or so later I wondered if he was right. I had climbed Soufrière, the great volcano that slumbers above Basse-Terre. Descending at dusk, lost, I found myself in a vast banana grove. All was silence. Then I heard the sound of drumming, and walked toward it until I found the drummer. He was young, and his drum was an empty crate; the rhythm I had heard before—along the Gulf of Guinea, very possibly in his ancestors' homeland.

He gave me a drink of water and directions. I asked who had taught him to drum in that way. "*Taught* me?" he asked in true astonishment. "My hands just *know*." As I left, he switched on a portable radio, and I was followed by the blare of American disco music, and I understood that I'd met a man who belonged effortlessly in two worlds.

"It is a new thing, to be proud of being colored," a Guadeloupian of mixed blood told me. "Here, we admire what you have done in America. We see that you have dealt with the racial question in a humane and rational way." My companion was Luc Michaux-Vignes, manager of American Airlines for Guadeloupe. "I could never have risen so high in a French company," he asserted. "The policy of the French is to have only French managers in this island. Oddly, there is no limit to how high a black Frenchman may rise in France—a man from Martinique is among the chief advisers to the President of the Republic —but here, the frontiers are sealed."

Such realities—and white Frenchmen deny their existence—have produced an emotional tide for "autonomy," a code word for independence.

Yet Guadeloupe has a two-crop economy, of sugar and bananas, the bananas grown mostly in the rugged highlands of Basse-Terre. Guadeloupe could not possibly sell these outside France at prices that would support the present standard of living. "There would be ten years of bitter sacrifice if the French go," a leftist theorist told me. "We cannot tell the people that, or they would abandon the cause."

Many streams converge in these folk, living on their fertile green islands, driving French cars, dancing to American music, searching for an African past, and peering through the mists of European political ideas toward a future that may prove costly in unexpected ways.

I think, often, of two things that

Roger Fortuné said. He told me that the single happiest moment of his life was in France, when he had first sipped Muscadet, seated in the sunlight by the tranquil waters of the Loire. Moments later he asked: "What if the ship carrying my slave forebears had been captured by the Spanish or the English or the Dutch? Would I not still be a man of the Caribbean? One day we will unite, from Curaçao to the Virgins—many cultures, one people!"

Meanwhile—ah, there is Martinique. It was an island inhabited only by women, as Columbus heard of it on his first voyage—women to whom Carib men came on occasion as lovers. Nothing of that tantalizing legend survives in the prosaic accounts of his landing there ten years later, after a decade of gazing upon paradise after paradise.

To the French, Martinique is the pearl of the Antilles, birthplace of the Empress Josephine, a fecund land in which poets and admirals, revolutionaries and beautiful women have grown as riotously as tropical flowers.

Like France herself, this is a land that longs for the painter's brush. Who but Cézanne would have attempted these fruits, who but John Singer Sargent captured the depthy black of these volcanic sand beaches? What would Utrillo have done with the mean streets of Fort-de-France, Watteau with the lush upland farms, Renoir with the sun which is the color of a young girl's blush, shining through the mists above Pelée, the volcano that killed 30,000 people in its great eruption in 1902?

Volcanic peaks give the island a dramatic terrain, nearly 5,000 feet at its highest; and rain forest covers much of the ranges. Only a few miles from the capital city of Fort-de-France, I found a fair valley screened on all sides by highland and watered by the Rivière Blanche. Here, at the Plantation Gabriel Régis, a family enterprise raises anthurium, porcelain rose, red ginger, bird of paradise, hibiscus—great odorless flowers in colors without any matching words. The bearded, husky manager, Jean-Gabriel-Régis, led me about. I seemed to have strayed into a landscape by Le Douanier Rousseau: I expected to see the great smiling moon face of a tiger, painted by a man who felt that nature might well have made its creatures more interesting.

"We pick 7,000 flowers a week for export, all grown on our ten hectares," Jean-Gabriel told me. "A mixed bouquet of 20 flowers sells to a tourist for 40 francs—about $10. Watch where you step—sometimes a fer-de-lance wanders in here, and it is a deadly serpent."

To grow a tree here, one simply thrusts a stake into the moist soil; within two weeks it puts down roots and puts out leaves. "But it must be a tree of this place, a gliricidia or a mahogany," said Jean-Gabriel. "European trees won't live here—our soil consumes their roots."

The cities are more assertive. On Guadeloupe, Pointe-à-Pitre is a little Marseilles. The capital of Martinique is a little Paris. One might be beside the Seine, the frocks are so fashionable, the restaurants so dear, the people so brusque. One day I remarked to an acquaintance that, lovely though the women may be and handsome the men, in my weeks on the island I had not seen any expression on these comely faces except a disgruntled frown. *That* elicited a laugh! "Ah," said he, "that's the famous Martinique smile!"

It doesn't mean a thing. Seldom have I met a more generous people. I was invited to party after party—and a party begins right after the shops close, and lasts until dawn. One dances the *biguine,* a hypnotic two-step done with the eyes and with the spine and its connecting bones, rather than with the feet. One drinks *'ti-ponch,* a potent mixture of syrup and the white Martinique rum. One talks and talks—and eats and eats.

I encountered a bespectacled rotund Frenchman *(Continued on page 133)*

osmopolitan charm of the French isles appears in Guadeloupe's bistros as well as Martinique's men of note. Poet and politician Aimé Césaire (right), mayor of Fort-de-France, drew worldwide recognition forty years ago for eloquently espousing négritude as an ideal akin to black pride. Mementos of Josephine surround veterinarian and amateur historian Dr. Robert Rose-Rosette inside La Pagerie, her childhood home, which he bought and has renovated as a museum.

Hugging the Martinique coast beneath volcanic Mont Pelée, St. Pierre belies its tragic

past. Pelée's eruption on May 8, 1902, obliterated the city known as "Paris of the Antilles."   131

With all the grace of a gently curving cutlass blade, charter yacht Sirocco knifes through the blue off Martinique's Caribbean shore. On board to enjoy the day's ideal sailing weather: author Charles McCarry and guests bound for the island's hilly southern tip.

at one such party, and he left off dancing long enough for a chat. He glowed with happiness. "I lived 28 years in Paris and never once had a good time," he told me. "Here, for five years, everyone has *insisted* that I enjoy myself. I am invited every night, and I always go." When, then, did he sleep? "Sleep? That is for people who live under gray skies and worry about life. One wants to be awake in a place like this."

A most hospitable couple, Yves and Monique Parfait, invited my wife, Nancy, and me, to a family party at their handsome house overlooking the harbor, the Baie de Fort-de-France. Amid the happy babble of children and grandchildren in three languages—French, Creole, and English, for some of the children were educated in America—we feasted through a whole sunny day.

Great trays of a special Martinique delicacy, *sang frit,* were passed with the first 'ti-ponch of the day. This dish, Yves explained, is made of the fresh blood of a steer, boiled until it congeals, seasoned with *piment féroce* (hot pepper) and other good things, and then fried in slices. It is delicious, like very delicate liver, and I said so. "It was better when we could get goat's blood," apologized Yves, "but that isn't so easy any more."

Many good things followed, ending with an enormous couscous, French cheese, French bread, French pastry. The cuisine, the perfect manners, the good lighthearted talk—all seemed to Nancy and me a wonderful mixture of two climates and two cultures.

Family matters can become very complex here. Island-born males emigrate to metropolitan France in greater numbers than do women; the males who stay may maintain as many as three separate households. On Sunday the "official" family gets together for a feast; the "unofficial" children are brought on other days to meet their paternal grandmother, who is usually quite as fond of them as of her legitimate descendants.

"It's considered manly and healthy for a man of Martinique to behave like this," I was told by Ruth de Thoré, a Dutchwoman who has been married to one. "Some have ten or twenty children. The mistresses want the youngsters because they love children and want something for themselves; they know the man will go away sooner or later. The bill is paid by social security—from Paris."

In Martinique there are three "native" peoples: the *béké,* who are of unmixed white blood, the descendants of early colonizers; those of mixed blood, who are often related to the béké; and those of unmixed African ancestry, who are often related to the mulattoes. Today, intermarriage is rare, but one family of mixed blood may contain representatives of all three colors. "You never know what you are going to get," a pregnant young woman told me, "but it is always a beautiful surprise."

We had various surprises in a rough sail to St. Barthélemy—St. Barts to all—with *Sirocco* close-hauled and pummeled by a boisterous sea that was running at six to eight feet. Normally under such conditions one is drenched with spray. That day the Caribbean came aboard in sheets. I was nearly knocked off the fantail by one gush of water that hit me so hard I thought for a moment that a big fish had leaped aboard and slapped me off my chair.

It was worth it. St. Barts is 10 square miles of steep arid hills and lovely coves with sparkling white sand beaches—and many official notices that nudism is prohibited. Still, on some beaches one might see *(Continued on page 141)*

Tourists seeking the good life often find it on Martinique's beaches, where they devote themselves to the sun, snorkeling, fishing, or other holiday pursuits. Hotels, such as the Bakoua pictured here, seldom rise higher than three stories, and palm trees surround them. Most of the Bakoua's guests come from Europe, enhancing the aura of sophistication that blends Gallic and Caribbean traditions. Excellent local restaurants offer continental or Creole cuisine accompanied by French wines and Martiniquan rums.

Afternoon glow plays over Grande Rivière, a fishing village on the northernmost point of Martinique. Residents of this isolated spot far from bustling Fort-de-France rely almost exclusively on gommiers (left)—long, open sailing craft named for the gum trees that provide the dugout hulls. These follow a design developed by the seagoing Carib Indians. Grande Rivière fishermen, renowned for their daring, range as far as 20 miles offshore to troll for tuna, king mackerel, dolphin, and other big fish, returning each evening to sell their catch on the beaches. Islanders also seine and hand-line for smaller fish, and set "eel pots" for reef fish, spiny lobsters and other shellfish, and moray eels.

Alone with the sea, a wind-surfer pilots his sail-mounted surfboard along Martinique's

palm-fringed shore near Ste-Anne, a village known for its fine white beaches.

bare-breasted girls from mainland France. Swimming or wind-surfing or sunbathing, a very pretty—and a very innocent—sight they make.

Apart from the tourists, who pour in by the thousand each year, and a resident expatriate community, there are two distinct populations in St. Barts. In the countryside, much intermarried, live the descendants of the hundred Normans and Bretons who settled here in 1659 to cultivate vegetables and tobacco. A second community resulted from a 93-year period of Swedish rule. France ceded St. Barts to Sweden in 1784 in return for trading rights in Göteborg. The capital was renamed Gustavia in honor of King Gustaf III, was declared a free port in 1785, and flourished under Swedish rule until 1877, when it was sold back to France for 320,000 francs.

Except for a few place-names, Swedish faded out long ago. French-speaking folk usually know the standard language, a dialect full of seafarer's idioms—a wrecked car is "scuttled," and a tethered cow is "moored"—and Creole, with words of African, French, Spanish, Dutch, or other origins. English was, and is, the language of Gustavia.

One of Gustavia's leading citizens, Marius Stakelborough, told me that an old pattern of linguistic separation persisted into his childhood. His parents spoke English only; when he went to school fifty years ago, he knew not a word of French, the official language of instruction. "I have taken care to speak French *and* English to all nine of my children, and two of them have lived in France," said Marius. "Of course they came back to St. Barts. We can go abroad, but when we return and see what we were foolish enough to leave behind, we cannot go away ever again."

Marius is proprietor of Le Select, a bar that is the social center of Gustavia; on the morning we met, he had been witness to the first wedding of a Swedish couple on St. Barts in two hundred years. Proud of his heritage, he displays a picture of himself with King Carl XVI Gustaf; the two men are grinning merrily at each other.

"They said in Stockholm, 'The king doesn't smile very much,'" Marius remembered. "But I said, 'Anyone who meets me has to smile.' I was invited for ten minutes and the king kept me for thirty. I invited him to St. Barts but I said, 'Come unofficially, Your Majesty—you'll have more fun!'"

Some topics take the smile from Marius's aquiline face with its white goatee. "St. Barts is moving too fast," he warned. "The young don't care. I care. The good days were when my children were small and all the island would come to Le Select at five for an apéritif. My wife would sit by the door and knit and we'd all talk—the teacher, the mayor, the policeman, the fisherman. You could catch all the fish and conch you wanted in the harbor. Now it's all polluted." He waved a hand at the harbor, where a hundred yachts lay at anchor among rainbows of leaking diesel fuel. "I have to follow up; I have built a bigger café. But I am sad."

From real-estate specialist Roger Lacour and his young American wife, Brook, I got an idea of the magnetism of the island: "If you wanted to build a house here, any architect you consulted would tell you there are ten people ahead of you." They quoted $50,000 for a half-acre inland site; I heard even higher prices. Various factors, including the need to import most materials, would make a three-bedroom house cost at least $150,000. *(Continued on page 146)*

Pulsing, nonstop tattoo of the tumba *throbs throughout Martinique's packed streets as Carnival revelers mass in a five-day-long frenzy of dance, masques, and parties that culminate with the effigy burning of Vaval, king of Carnival, and the arrival of Lent.*

Mirroring her island's
unique past, a matron
of St. Barthélemy—"St.
Barts"—wears its pleated,
starched calèche, or
cotton bonnet, a legacy from
Norman and Breton settlers
of the 1640's. Her fingers fly as
she plaits straw for a hat,
a famous item of local
craftswomen. Trim homes
separated by low stone walls—
and an absolute lack of neon—

convey a sense of provincial
France. Ceded to Sweden in
1784, bought back a century
later, St. Barts preserves
touches of Scandinavia. Its
population remains almost
entirely fair-skinned; terrain
too steep for sugar production
meant a limited need for slaves.

Tropic ease of St. Barts supplies decor for the wedding of two Parisians who choose a setting out of the ordinary. After the civil ceremony at Gustavia's city hall, Dante Larcade and bride Françoise Ville stroll through town to church (above); by special request their guests wear white, the men sporting straw boaters. All smiles after the religious rites, the wedding party goes to a reception, where Count Edouard de Moustier and his Countess—stepfather and mother of the bridegroom—join in a family portrait. The Count, a descendant of the Bourbons, has homes on Guadeloupe and St. Barts; his ancestors include a diplomat accredited to the United States during George Washington's lifetime.

On the other hand, there are no yearly taxes on real estate, and in practice—apart from a 3 percent impost on imported goods—no other taxes. The islanders are, in law, subject to income taxes, but only businessmen who cannot conceal *all* of their income will pay.

Smuggling has always been the heart's blood of St. Barts' economy. For the locals, it is perfectly legal—in a free port, they can sell liquor and tobacco and almost everything else cheaper than anyone in the Caribbean. If some traders prefer to load these items at night into shallow-draft boats with the hulls painted black—well, that is an eccentricity to be tolerated. The goods are run ashore in English-speaking islands. French islands are too well policed, apparently, to make the risk worthwhile.

Smugglers have long-standing business arrangements in St. Barts, and unquestioned credit. One legendary runner of contraband charged a thousand dollars' worth of gear in the local chandlery when I happened to be there. "You can count on him to pay," said the clerk on duty, "because you can count on him not to be caught."

At last we reached St. Martin, the last of the French Antilles. Again it was an exhilarating sail, *Sirocco* making eight and ten knots in seas that ran up to ten feet. Caleb, securing the staysail, was nearly flung overboard when the boat suddenly dropped out from under him; he hung onto the sheet with three feet of air beneath his own bare soles.

We reached Philipsburg, the harbor of the Dutch side, at dusk. I recognized the squat cylinders of storage tanks for oil and water, the concrete shells of raw construction, and the other monuments of northern civilization. It was as though the sea had in one great final convulsion spilled us out of paradise and onto the cold slab of the real world.

I had one more undertaking to fulfill before I said farewell to this "flawed portrait" of my beloved France. Nancy and I left the one garish bustling street of Philipsburg, lined with tax-free shops, glittering with consumer goods, and motored over to Grand Case. There, a few miles beyond the unattended border, on the French side of this divided island, we would have a final dinner at Chez Christophine.

Throughout the French islands we ate well. We had *boudin*, the fiery sausage of the islands, and dishes entirely worthy of their native Paris. But nowhere on the planet have we eaten better than in the little restaurant of Christophine Knight. Her *crabe farci*, her *langouste à la créole* are summits of gastronomy. She learned to cook at age five, she told me, standing on a box at a wood-burning stove. Her teacher was a great celebrity on St. Martin, Madame Chance, who owned this restaurant before Christophine and her husband, Wilmot, took it over. As Madame Chance's Cockfight Arena and Sporting House, it was famous for its conch-and-goat stew, which unhappily is no longer on the menu.

Christophine is a majestic woman, well over six feet tall, with bones well covered by flesh the hue of an aubergine. As she stood by our table chatting, I overheard a Frenchwoman nearby exclaiming, "Wouldn't Gauguin have loved to have painted that woman!"

Ah, no, I thought—Christophine, with her skin so full of light and her face so lit by her humanity, was beyond human skill, even beyond genius. God kept Christophine's color—and all the colors of these enchanted isles—for His own palette.

6 | North to the Leewards

Written by Charles McCarry and photographed by Jodi Cobb

Day's end catches a thunderhead crowning Montserrat, one of the least developed of the Antilles. Columbus discovered it in 1493, naming it for a mountain-girt monastery near Barcelona. Its lack of good harbors hampered settlers after 1632, when persecuted Irish Catholics from St. Kitts found refuge here. Place-names such as Kinsale and Galway's Estate survive; so do a local brogue and a nickname, Emerald Isle of the Caribbean.

As Dominica's misty mountains rose off *Sirocco*'s bow in late afternoon, my son Caleb, on watch as helmsman while the rest of us snoozed, suddenly cried out: "Dolphins! All *right!*"

In an instant we were awake, laughing in delight and calling to the school of frolicking porpoises that swam alongside. We were making eight knots. For our cousins from the deep, this was idling speed, and they leapt from the water, their sleek bodies shining, as if to return our greeting.

Too soon, they fell behind, perhaps to snack on one of the schools of flying fish we had seen scattered over the water like pieces of eight. "Come back!" called Jodi Cobb. "We love you!" But within moments they were far astern.

We did not know for certain what lay ahead of us on Dominica—we were sailing into a storm center. Just recently, Patrick John had been forced to resign as Prime Minister after his Defence Force had fired on a public demonstration in Roseau, the capital. A two-week general strike had paralyzed the feeble economy and the beleaguered government of the island. Jodi remarked that her Caribbean assignment had called for photographing four heads of government—of these, three were already out of office and one had died.

Since then, more profound changes have taken place. The Dominica we saw has literally vanished. On August 29, 1979, in one of the greatest natural disasters on record in this part of the world, Hurricane David struck Dominica with winds as strong as 150 miles per hour. Forty-two people were killed, perhaps 2,000 hurt, 60,000 left homeless as two-thirds of the buildings were wrecked.

The hurricane destroyed 100 percent of the bananas, maybe 80 percent of the coconut crop—leaving palms scattered like jackstraws—and like percentages of the citrus, cacao, mango, and breadfruit trees. Eight out of ten fishing boats were lost. Roseau lay in splinters, roofs stripped from the sturdiest buildings. Strong new port facilities had been crumpled. Everyone agreed it would take years, perhaps an entire generation, to return Dominica even to what she had been—a place, as one young Dominican told me, "where there are no 'haves' or 'have-nots,' because here we are all 'have-nots' together."

Yet there was hope. On our arrival in mid-July, Dominica rang with exultant discussion. Free at last of the discredited John regime, this newly independent nation believed that it could be governed by honest leaders, that it could take a prideful place in its region and the world, and that it could, by intelligent planning, bring a measure of security and prosperity to its impoverished people. If brains and idealism could have accomplished these things, then they would surely have been done, for I have never encountered in any other place so many brilliant young people, animated by a love of country and a belief in its future, as I met here.

Perhaps they took inspiration from the mountain landscape, often called the loveliest in the Caribbean. We saw it first from the Martinique Passage. Dominica is said to have 365 rivers, one for every day of the year, and streams sparkled in the sun. In her high forests, a perpetual rain comes down, and as the light shone through these mists, we had the illusion that *Sirocco* was sailing into a rainbow. We moored by the light of a full moon that hung between two inky peaks.

Next day, we drove to Trafalgar Falls, twin cataracts about five miles inland. On a dreadful road, we found ourselves with an escort of fleet young

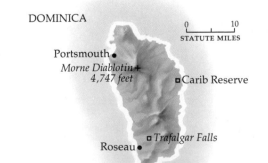

DOMINICA

0   10
STATUTE MILES

Portsmouth•
Morne Diablotin+
4,747 *feet*
□Carib Reserve

□*Trafalgar Falls*
Roseau•

boys. Magically, they emerged from the forest, and on bare feet they sped by our lumbering vehicle. When we parked at a modest restaurant, we understood: These lads—the whole nimble, voluble, grinning platoon of them—wanted to be our guides. They would carry our gear and show us the way for one dollar "E.C.," Eastern Caribbean currency, or 37 cents U. S. My companion, a knobby 14-year-old called Damian (how the poetry of Christendom sings in these island names!), laid a gentle fingertip on the leaves of a mimosa. They shrank from his touch and closed. "Sensitive plant," Damian told me with a scholarly air. He steered me around a large land crab, brownish-orange of shell, that waved its formidable claws like an old-time, bare-knuckle boxer.

The falls, two veils of light on the face of a cliff, were surrounded by a rain forest so green that to stand in it was like being inside the eye of a cat. Damian pointed to the higher cascade, then to the other. "The father and the mother," said he with a grin. "For once, the father is more beautiful." Caleb "showered" under the larger cascade, and the icy water knocked the breath from his lungs. The pool at the base, heated by thermal springs, was much warmer. With a sailor's cry of joy, Captain Jim Steivang plunged in downstream to soak the salt from his pores; his ten-year-old guide Stephen lathered himself freely with Jim's shaving cream, dived under the rushing surface, and came up again sleek as an otter. And then we went on to Roseau. *(Continued on page 161)*

As a unit, the Dutch "3-S" group— Sint Maarten, Saba, and Statia—shares equal status with each of the ABC's in the Kingdom of the Netherlands. Dutch usage calls the 3-S isles "Windward," the ABC's "Leeward."

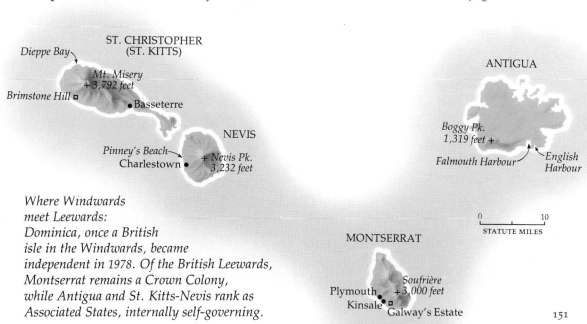

Where Windwards meet Leewards: Dominica, once a British isle in the Windwards, became independent in 1978. Of the British Leewards, Montserrat remains a Crown Colony, while Antigua and St. Kitts-Nevis rank as Associated States, internally self-governing.

151

A nation is born: On November 3, 1978—exactly 485 years after Columbus discovered Dominica—the island celebrates independence with a festival of rallies, punch parties, speeches, and pageants. His gauntleted arms swinging smartly despite the rain, cadet lieutenant Francis Richards leads a parade. Revelers in and out of costume crowd the streets of Roseau, the capital, beneath the fledgling nation's newly adopted symbol, the Sisserou or imperial parrot. Mountainside forests that sheltered the bird constituted a major national resource for a populace of 80,000. Citizens' smiles reflect the reigning mood: joyful hopes of a better future for the island, one of the Caribbean's poorest.

"**H**andsome, well-shaped people . . . graceful enough," a 17th-century writer called the Carib Indians, then a people of war. Today, some 2,000 Caribs make their homes in a 3,700-acre reserve on Dominica, living by farming, fishing, and basket-weaving. Above, the author's guide Abraham John and his sister Nydia Lockhart meet at one family house; at another, Christine Valmond cuddles her daughter Ursula. Rugged and thinly settled, this island kept much of the natural beauty their ancestors knew; hundreds of streams lace its slopes, with cascades and cataracts as dramatic as Trafalgar Falls (opposite).

155

Devastation rules Dominica in the wake of Hurricane David. Fifty-foot seas and 150-mile-an-hour winds slashed at the island on August 29, 1979, denuding the once-lush slopes behind the Botanical Gardens (above) at Roseau, uprooting vast tracts of forest and causing massive erosion, flattening the vital banana crop, and wrecking a predominantly agricultural economy. David virtually demolished Roseau, gutting such sturdy structures as the semicircular Fort Young Hotel and the Anglican Church (left); it completely obliterated flimsier homes. It killed at least 42 people and left 60,000 homeless. Survivors found themselves without power, communications, safe water, or adequate food. Relief organizations and countries around the world responded quickly to the emergency, but normality remained a distant prospect. Catastrophic in its timing as well as its force, the storm hit Dominica only three months after a prolonged political crisis stemming from charges of corruption among top officials. An interim government had taken charge peacefully and legally; its prospects seemed bright—until the hurricane struck.

*F*riendliness lives up to an island's
reputation in the household of
Montserratian farmer James Duberry
and his wife, Margaret, with their
granddaughter Junie. Like his neighbor

Mrs. Peter Cabey (top left), he raises tomatoes and other produce, including cucumbers, beans, onions, sweet potatoes, cabbage. With help from the United Nations, Montserrat works toward higher yields in foodstuffs. Under proper transport and marketing arrangements, its crops could become a major export to nearby islands and even to Canada or the United Kingdom. Bananas, grown on a small scale, meet the local demand.

"The government of Patrick John fell because it was corrupt, incompetent, and morally blind!" With that peppery summary, a bright, witty, bespectacled young woman named Marie-Elena ("Mena") Boyd began to explain recent events. On Bloody Tuesday, May 29, Mena Boyd was among the demonstrators gathered near Government Headquarters in protest. John's government had introduced bills that would have limited the freedom to strike and effectively ended freedom of the press. Instead, his administration collapsed.

The interim Prime Minister, Oliver James Seraphin, and I met over a glass of ginger ale to discuss the perils and temptations facing the new "mini-states" of the Caribbean. Mr. Seraphin summed these up in vivid language. "In the days after independence," he said, "Dominica was like a young virgin going into the bars for the first time. The wolves— there were rumors that criminals from abroad had an interest in this country— gathered around."

And now?

"The earth-shaking thing," Mr. Seraphin added, "is that the government has been changed by constitutional *and* revolutionary means. John was brought down by a coalition of his own former ministers and the opposition, acting on the will of the people. The transition has been orderly and peaceful."

The Prime Minister had generously taken time for me on the eve of a mini-summit with the new leaders of Grenada and St. Lucia. I asked if a political orientation like theirs might be expected in Dominica. Mr. Seraphin thought before he spoke. "One may be ideologically indisposed to accept aid from a certain country; but if your people are in need, and food and medicine are offered, you cannot say no. If the United States does not help, these islands will turn to others." Namely Cuba? "I do not like to say that," he replied.

After Hurricane David struck, there were rumors that a contingent of Cubans—including some troops to "keep order"—had headed for Dominica. An international relief effort had already been welcomed; it included British, French, Barbadian, and Venezuelan personnel as well as an emergency-repair team of American Seabees. Dominicans made a colorful comment about the prospect of the Cubans: A local shop happened to have a large supply of red-white-and-blue fabric, Stars and Stripes material left over from the Bicentennial. Lengths of it were cut up, streamers of it were strung over the battered streets of Roseau, and ruined buildings flew their improvised Old Glory by the score.

"We would have flown the flag of almost any country as a sign of protest," one Dominican explained. "In any case, the flags made the wishes of many people clear: No Cuban troops were wanted here, and none came."

Men have been contending for the land, and for ideas, and for customs, for centuries in these islands. No people fought more fiercely than those for whom the Caribbean is named: the Carib Indians. In pre-Columbian times, they had left the South American coast and subdued a gentler race, the Arawak, who had settled the islands before them. They killed the Arawak men, devouring many, and took the women to wife; for generations Carib men kept a vocabulary of their own while females spoke a language essentially Arawakan.

The Caribs greeted Columbus with a shower of poisoned arrows on first sight in 1493. Their greeting to other Europeans was *(Continued on page 166)*

Soundproof glass reflects pop singer Jimmy Buffett as support vocalists Keith Sykes and Deborah McColl dub harmony in a recording studio on Montserrat. Buffett's easygoing, bittersweet songs of island life underline his prolonged love affair with the Caribbean.

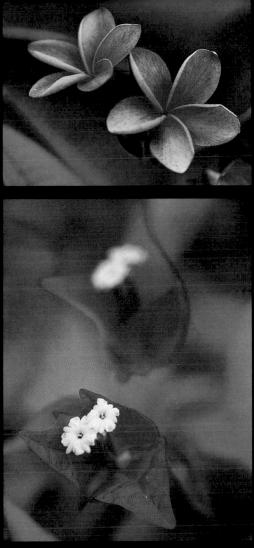

Legacy of tropical sun and moist trade winds, the Caribbean's
lush flora brightens all but the most arid islands with a kaleidoscope
of colors, shapes, and perfumes. Great estates and modest houses gain
charm from this bounty. Hibiscus (opposite, top and far left) originated
in China. A sturdy shrub, the coral plant bears delicate flowers in clusters
(left) as wide as ten inches. Frangipani—used in religious rites by the
Maya and the Aztec Indians—puts forth intensely fragrant blossoms
of yellow, white, red, or pink (top). Bougainvillea's flowering vines (above),
sometimes trimmed into shrubs, scale hillsides and tall trees, draping

E ye-catching spinnakers balloon before the wind in a 35-mile-long yacht race during Antigua's annual Sailing Week. One couple tries wind-surfing—riding a sail-equipped surfboard—in Falmouth Harbour. Sailing Week's less formal events include a Wet T-Shirt Competition, a Rubber Dinghy Tug-of-War, and a Non-Mariners' Race, in which homemade "vessels" compete for speed, originality, and carrying capacity (below).

Antigua's star-shaped Middle Ground juts between distant Falmouth Harbour and yacht-strewn English Harbour, a superbly sheltered anchorage. Pleasure craft tie up at Nelson's Dockyard—a restoration today, a base for fighting ships in the 18th century.

pretty much the same. They massacred all but a few of the first settlers of St. Barts in 1656, and elsewhere made ferocious raids on white colonizers.

The last substantial group of Island Caribs lives on a reserve perched on a mountainside on the northeast shoulder of Dominica. Abraham John, a small-boned man as quick and as quiet as a forest creature, volunteered to accompany Jodi Cobb and me on a visit to his people. Like many of them, and like some other rural Dominicans for that matter, Abraham is fluent only in Creole. "Only very, very old Caribs know words of our own language," he said. "It has almost flown away forever."

The old skills have not, happily, flown away. The first sight that greeted us in the reserve was a dugout canoe, still raw from the ax. Carib fishermen launch such boats into the wild sea that beats against the rocks on this shore, and return with fish for the table. Elsewhere we saw intricate baskets woven from coarse grasses. Jodi bought one, and the woman who had made it gave her a pineapple as a present, to keep hospitality unviolated.

There will be no shortage of Caribs in generations to come. We found Alfred and Jeannine Frederick, kindred of Abraham's, in their dooryard. Alfred held three small children in his lap. I asked about the family. "Six we have," said Jeannine. "Twenty we'll make. We agreed on that." Carib style, they live in two houses—a big one made of lumber as a social center and a cookhouse smudged with charcoal smoke.

Again and again, we met Abraham's nephews and cousins, sisters and brothers. With affectionate greetings went a handful of cigarettes, and coins for those troops of children tagging along—eyes black as kohl, smiles bright

as stars, and bellies distended by a diet deficient in protein. It was impossible to see beyond these gentle, quiet people into their bloody history. "They are very good," remarked Eden, our black driver. "They love each other."

Next day, sailing up the leeward coast, we aboard *Sirocco* saw that at least one tropical legend is true. Many had spoken to me—some with skepticism—of the "Green Flash," a brief emerald glimmer that sometimes appears on the horizon at sunset. Jim Steivang, Mark Meyers, Caleb McCarry, and I attest that at 6:32 p.m. on Saturday, July 14, the sun descended through a layer of cirrus and then, a great red disk, dropped like a stone into the sea. The Green Flash drew an emerald line on the eyelid of the horizon—and the vanished sun sent up an afterlight with rays of blue and salmon, like the ribs of a fan.

We visited Portsmouth, Dominica's second city (population perhaps 3,000 before Hurricane David), and young men in homemade boats came alongside *Sirocco*, hawking everything from fresh fruit to tours up the Indian River. Caleb and I decided on a tour with a voluble 20-year-old named George Tavernier.

George is whippet-slender, with muscles as taut as a stretched sail. He rows the mile upriver and back, with an additional mile or so in the strong harbor swell, and charges $1.85 U. S. for the trip. He can earn $7.50 a day in tourist season. By Portsmouth standards he is well-to-do; laborers should get a minimum wage of $1.92 a day, and they are lucky to work two or three days a week. "We eat the things that grow, and they always grow," said George. "It's a good thing. We'd all be crazy people otherwise." After Hurricane David, of course, many things grew no more.

168

History lingers on St. Kitts' Brimstone Hill, called "Gibraltar of the West Indies" for its own shape and its imposing fort (left). In 1782, outnumbered British defenders endured a month-long siege by 6,000 French before surrendering; the French already held Statia (on the horizon, left); but a naval victory off Dominica rescued the British cause in the Indies. Warfare between France and Britain made St. Kitts a frequent battleground in the 17th and 18th centuries. Today, local antiques and contemporary West Indian art decorate the Golden Lemon (below and lower left), a hotel in a renovated house—once a shipping merchant's—at Dieppe Bay.

Along the Indian River, a shallow murky stream lined with mangroves, he told me a popular rumor: that magic had brought down the John administration. On Good Friday, it was said, a voodoo woman with a white fowl in her arms arrived at the airport—possibly from Guyana, possibly from Guadeloupe— and a car took her to the house of a high official of government.

"This man drank blood from that fowl and ate its meat on Good Friday, and that's why his fall came. Voodoo and the Savior were *both* angry, and there was too much power against him."

George Tavernier is a fervent Christian and a diligent man. "I believe in the Savior," he said, "but voodoo works."

Beyond the Guadeloupe Passage, a very different isle lay ahead: unmysterious Montserrat. One steps ashore here into a well-kept garden. Flowers and trees are the same as on other islands, but the colors are muted, the sizes less extravagant. The very sun, it seemed to me, was paler and less insistent.

Montserrat, according to legend, is the island that gave the English a pungent nickname. I came across a story— not highly historical—that the limes which checked scurvy on British warships were first grown here. A debatable tradition has it that the locals speak with an Irish brogue, the legacy of early

settlers; and a stronger tradition claims Montserrat as hospitality's own island.

"The first thing a Montserratian will do is ask you into his home," barrister Kenneth Allen told me. "No matter how simple his house or how plain his food, he will want to share it. If you are a king or a pauper doesn't matter—he will assume that you will like what he has and enjoy yourself. And you will."

How right Kenneth Allen was. At his hillside home overlooking the harbor, Caleb and I munched delicious island specialties prepared by Edith Allen, now the director of tourism. We enjoyed delightful talk. Everyone present seemed to be a *(Continued on page 178)*

Mourners gather at St. George's Anglican Church on May 29, 1979, for the funeral of Paul Southwell, first Chief Minister of St. Kitts and Nevis, and an ardent champion of Caribbean unity. Today, one parliament rules St. Kitts and its less-developed sister, Nevis, where small farms and tranquil vistas like Pinney's Beach remain the rule, not the exception. Here Alexander Hamilton was born; and Capt. Horatio Nelson of the Royal Navy wooed and married Fanny Nisbet. Ruins of once-elegant mansions and an 18th-century bathhouse evoke Nevis' heyday as a fashionable mineral spa.

Straining fishermen heave their boat ashore on Sint Eustatius, where the derelict timbers of an old pier sprout like totems from dark volcanic sands. This quiet Dutch island—usually called Statia—once held one of the busiest free ports in the Caribbean. Sugar, slaves, and much of the war matériel needed by America's rebellious thirteen colonies passed through here. Contraband trade became so profitable that Statia's wealth earned it the nickname "Golden Rock." In November 1776, it saluted the American warship Andrew Doria—the first time a foreign power had formally honored a vessel of the Continental Navy. Britain punished this and other improprieties by seizing the island, auctioning off its vast stores of supplies, and sacking the port. Broken clay pipes (left, above), made at Gouda in the Netherlands in 1746 or shortly thereafter, recall Statia's earliest enterprise—Dutch tobacco plantations that sold leaf in the homeland by 1638.

*H*alf and half: Dutch Sint Maarten and French St. Martin divide the 33 square miles of a single island. Widened by recent landfills, Philipsburg—capital of the Dutch portion— clings to a sandspit between its yacht-flecked harbor and its Great Salt Pond. Salt first drew Dutch settlers here in the 1630's; although some production continues, tourism now provides the major industry, creating about 70 percent of local jobs. Casinos and duty-free shops lure seasonal visitors, while unspoiled vistas encourage construction of such luxurious homes as the William Nichols residence (left) near the French capital, Marigot.

Sabans in holiday finery celebrate Palm Sunday: Cornelia Jones bends down to joke with Veronica Wilson and Kevin and Lisa Johnson. Residents worship at Catholic, Wesleyan Holiness, or Anglican services. Dutch by nationality, the "3-S" islanders grow up speaking English; British settlers followed pioneering Hollanders to Saba in the 1650's. Rugged and beachless, this five-square-mile mountain-peak isle favored resolute defenders—they could drop rocks on would-be invaders. Since World War II, jeep-worthy roads have replaced stone steps that once linked tiny towns, seacoast, and lush uplands.

Renaissance man or woman—Kenneth is a songwriter and musician as well as a lawyer; his friend Howard Fergus, Speaker of the House, is a noted poet. "I have had a frantic week, because the Governor has been away and I have been Acting Governor as well as Speaker," he told me. "All the time I felt a poem gestating. Today I had an hour to bring it forth, and I must say I feel better!"

Here the future was discussed in measured terms. "I am not so certain that independence is the best course right now, although I have pushed it in the past," said Howard Fergus. "I have been out in the country, talking to the people. They are uninterested. The elderly have a sentimental attachment to England—and of course, there is the money. Britain pays about one-tenth of our budget."

"All that fuming in the U.N. about colonialism embarrasses the British," said Ivan Browne, a professional singer who is also an accountant and who decided, in middle age, to study law. "It seems sensible to us to go on as a colony, but the British may very well want out of it. They have to accept slander in world forums to keep us as we are. It's hardly a fair exchange for them, is it?"

Montserrat's climate, of weather as of opinion, seems more temperate than that of other islands. Plymouth, the shady capital, has the hushed air of an English village. In former times, sea-island cotton and limes were the cash crops here, but young people have no great mind to work the land. Yet the cotton may have a future.

In an airy workshop near Fort Barrington I called on a Nova Scotian, Mrs. Clara Davidson, resident tutor at the Montserrat Weaving Studio. Twelve girls, chattering happily above the clack of their looms, were busy weaving. Mrs. Davidson handed me an attractive purse made of sea-island cotton grown, spun, and woven on Montserrat. "We sold work worth about $15,000 E.C. right from our shop in the first quarter of

1979," she told me. "I came here six years ago on holiday with my sons, and they told me I ought to come back and *do* something for Montserrat. So I came.

"Under a grant from the Canadian government, the island will get 112 new looms by the end of 1980, the Montserratians will be doing my job, and I shall go back to Nova Scotia. And whenever I see our sea-island work in shops in London, or wherever I am, I'll return in my memory to Montserrat."

Another new industry has been imported by a genial Englishman named George Martin. Caleb recognized that name instantly: the producer of all but one of the albums of the Beatles. George has installed a complete recording facility, Air Studios Montserrat, on a hilltop above Plymouth. Showing us around, he played a few rippling bars on a piano, coaxed a chord or two from a Moog synthesizer, explained the complicated soundproofing—polished ash floors to reflect some frequencies, rough stone walls and hollowed ceilings to absorb or diffuse others. He whipped the plastic cover from the "desk," a control panel 15 feet long that can "hear," modulate, mix, and record 46 separate tracks of sound. I felt that I had made landfall in the 22nd century.

"It's not so complicated as it looks," said George, twirling dials as he spoke. "This [*click*] controls the channel, this [*twirl*] the sound. You fiddle with these, you see, to create the 'screen.'" The screen? "Yes, the whole wall in front of you is speakers all the way across. You can *move* parts of the sound. If I said, 'I want to move the guitars to that side of the cowbell,' why, I'd just adjust this control and move it over. You build up a 'picture,' and that becomes the record, you see."

My mind, which had been contemplating the age of sail, did not quite see, but could admire. As for Caleb, *he* was in the presence of history, not of what seemed to me the far-out future.

With every mile northward the sea

grew darker, and the waters round Redonda, a flint hatchet of an uninhabited isle jutting from the sea on our course to Nevis, were as black as Odyssean wine. A cloud of gulls, rising from Redonda's cliffs, called out to *Sirocco* in rowdy admiration, but she sailed on with hardly a toss of her flowing ensign.

Nevis, a volcanic cone of 36 steep square miles, has had poignant roles in history. Here in the 1750's, Alexander Hamilton was born, the illegitimate son of a bankrupt Scot and a willful island girl. In 1787, Horatio Nelson married a Nevis belle, the young widow Frances (Fanny) Nisbet, in a mansion now vanished. A church near Charlestown, the capital, proudly displays the record of Captain Nelson's marriage.

A strait two miles wide separates Nevis from her larger neighbor, St. Christopher, invariably called St. Kitts. Lofty St. Kitts, wearing a scarf of cloud and a ruffle of surf, is called by the British the mother isle of the West Indies. It was here they first settled, in 1624, and colonists soon set forth from St. Kitts for other islands. With Nevis, she forms an Associated State linked to Britain. In theory this used to include Anguilla, about 60 miles northward; in practice Anguilla, with a constitution of her own, has a special standing under the Crown. When the three-island state was established in 1967, Anguilla seceded. To stabilize matters, Britain finally made a show of force—two frigates, a contingent of paratroopers, even a party of London bobbies. Anguillans, 6,000 strong, explained with dignity that they loved the mother country as they could never love St. Kitts, and eventually were taken back into the bosom of Britannia.

St. Kitts in the times of slavery was among the most important agricultural islands in the Caribbean. It still is. On Nevis I encountered an old-time planter named Norman Maynard, who told me why. "St. Kitts has lovely soil, lovely," he said, and the tone of his voice suggested that he might be crumbling a handful of it as he spoke. He has constructed a working model of one of those wind-powered mills whose ruins stand all through the islands. Within living memory, some Caribbean sugar was processed in such mills, and Mr. Maynard, who began his career in 1918, knows just how it was done.

"The vanes are called 'points' locally, and they were covered with sailcloth. Each morning, first thing, the vanes were pointed into the wind and that would turn the shaft. The shaft was the best hardwood, usually greenheart; nothing else was strong enough to take the strain. The shaft rotated these three great metal rollers. The men fed the cane between these, and the juice was squeezed out. The cane fiber was burned to heat the huge coppers in which the juice was cooked for crystallized sugar and molasses. The molasses, of course, was turned into rum."

Mr. Maynard paused with a hand on his model, which works just as its original, twelve times larger, did. "Fortunes were made from sugar, you know," he said. "But not by those who got it done, the sugar-making."

That point is still valid. St. Kitts' past and its future, its economy and its politics, can be summarized in a single word: sugar. Ninety-two percent of its agricultural production and 75 percent of all its exports are sugar. Forty percent of the labor force—about 5,500 people out of a population of some 36,000—are employed in growing and processing sugar. Cane was first planted here in the 17th century. Until the end of the 18th century, when Britain began her campaign against the slave trade, cane formed the apex of that sinister triangle: Slaves cultivated sugar, sugar made rum in New England, slaves were bought in Africa for rum and transported to the islands to produce more sugar.

To labor in the canefield is to work as hard as human beings can be made to. I visited a field in St. Kitts during the harvest. This island—where feral monkeys live in a towering wild interior, and every inch of coastal land is under the plow—has the hardship of the tropics. The sun slaps the skull like a callused palm striking the head of a drum. The cane grows in close-set clumps ten feet high. Each clump is a miniature jungle, with the hazard of insects and rats, but not, on St. Kitts, venomous snakes.

Using the knife locally called a matchet, each cutter must chop the cane at the base, trim the leafy top, cut the stalks into convenient lengths, stack these to be loaded mechanically, and strew the debris aside. A cane cutter on St. Kitts earns $1.95 (U. S.) per ton. An average man can cut three tons in a day; an exceptional man, five tons. The harvest lasts from January to July; the annual wage of an average cutter fully employed could be, with bonuses, $935.86.

The government of St. Kitts took over the sugar industry in 1972 when private plantation operators found that banks would no longer advance them money. William Dore, dynamic chief of the National Agricultural Corporation, told me with pride of a leap in production to 40,000 tons a year, from a low of almost 24,000 in 1973.

"But," he went on, "it costs St. Kitts, which produces sugar about as cheaply as any other country in the Caribbean, over $350 to produce one ton. The world market price is about $300. Britain buys 15,000 tons of our sugar at a subsidized rate higher than the world price. We must sell the rest for less than it costs to put it aboard ship."

One young man I ran into expressed a familiar dilemma: "The government and the union work hand in hand. The union delivers the votes on which a Labour government stands or falls. Decisions are not made on a scientific basis, but by a bunch of politicians for reasons of survival."

Even Mr. Dore has wondered if St. Kitts can survive. "We are a social powder keg," he told me. "So far we have escaped the fate of Grenada and St. Lucia and Dominica. But how much longer can we do so?"

As he spoke, an assistant brought him the news that the price of gasoline for the sugar industry's tractors and trucks had risen overnight from $1.12 a gallon to $1.37. "St. Kitts is one of the poorest countries in the world, and the United States is the richest—but it would cost us that much more to sell you a pound of sugar."

Mr. Dore pointed out that the U. S. had failed to ratify the International Sugar Agreement which would regulate the world market, controlling prices and production. "How much you could help us," he sighed, "if you saw our value as clearly as the Cubans see Grenada's!"

I remembered the opinions of a young foreigner on St. Lucia, who had dined with us aboard *Sirocco*. What the people of the islands want, said this observer, is a better life and a freer voice— liberation from the capitalism that has ruled these islands ever since the first Europeans brought in the first slaves to grow the first sugar, the first bananas, the first sea-island cotton. And, most of all, equality and democracy. "Nothing will stop them, you know," he concluded. "They're ready to take it. It is no longer a matter of *giving*—to give a man what is his by right of birth is an insult."

The words of these two men rang in my memory a few days later. On Sunday morning I drove around St. Kitts, through streets silent save for the swelling choruses of hymns that issued from innumerable churches. Then I lunched at a posh hotel on the northern coast. Inside, all was fine wine and gracious service, and the gay small talk of the idle. A woman with a voice full of money told her tablemates how her plastic surgeon had recently tightened her buttocks. "I had to lie on my tummy sipping martinis through a straw for weeks, darlings! But now heads turn when I wear my French jeans on Fifth Avenue!"

Outside, beyond a wall covered

with flowers, people in their clean and modest best were walking home from church, scattering scrawny chickens underfoot in the dirt streets. In a good year, the men could earn enough money in the cane to spend a week in this exquisite small hotel. How long, indeed, can such an empire of dispassion endure?

The idea of empire lasted for a very long time in the Caribbean, with British men-of-war under such as Horatio Nelson and French fleets commanded by such as l'Amiral Comte de Grasse pounding ships of the line to splinters and bombarding shore installations during the 18th century and through the Napoleonic wars. De Grasse, badly defeated off the Iles des Saintes in 1782 by a British squadron under Sir George Rodney, has kept his prominence in history—he had commanded the French fleet that vanquished the English at the Chesapeake in the decisive naval battle of the American Revolution. Brimstone Hill, a colossal stone fortification guarding the leeward approaches of St. Kitts, is a reminder—as sharp as any I heard from buoyant radicals or from traditionalists with sinking hearts—that events on remote bits of real estate can be forerunners of upheavals that change the course of history.

Clearly visible from Brimstone Hill, the volcanic heights of Statia break the skyline. Formally named Sint Eustatius in the Dutch Bovenwindse or Windward group, it has twelve square miles, some 1,500 people, a litter of great masonry blocks at the water's edge as tokens of a once-thriving port. As good neutrals, the Dutch authorities exchanged salutes in 1776 with an American brigantine; after Britain declared war on the Netherlands, Admiral Rodney arrived with a fleet and sacked the island. Statia, the "Golden Rock," was despoiled by English guns and English greed.

With some of *Sirocco*'s crew, Caleb and I tried body-surfing on the windward shore. A girl weaving hibiscus into her long black hair warned us of undertow—"But you're sailors, you'll know." We waded into breakers that were as frisky as puppies and not much larger. Then the water was suddenly thirty feet deep and boiling. I was smashed against the sandy bottom, dragged toward Africa, tumbled and choked and slammed about. At last I was safe in six inches of water, like my companions. Resting, staring wearily up at a sheer dark cliff, I saw white specks moving about. By squinting I identified them as goats, hundreds of them, browsing on whatever vegetation clings limpet-like to the impassive rock.

Northwestward a few hours, more goats watched Jim Steivang nonchalantly bring *Sirocco* through a choppy sea to Saba's new pier. Saba has about 950 people, and most of them seemed there to greet us. I tossed out a mooring line, and the man who deftly caught the wind-whipped hemp turned out to be Stevanis Heiligher, the daring boatman who had brought ashore many visitors over the years. We boarded his groaning minibus to ride to the top of this precipitous cone. I started to introduce myself. "I know—you're Mr. McCarry," he said; "we heard you were coming on *Sirocco*." How? Stevanis just grinned, and so did we—word of us had flown ahead from island to island throughout the voyage. Gossip hangs over these ingrown places like the gulls above the harbors.

At noon precisely we arrived at the valley-sheltered village called The Bottom, a cluster of white cottages. We found a hotel, ordered a cold drink, and asked about sandwiches. "No," said the dour black Saban behind the bar. And that was that. One must make reservations by 10 a.m. for lunch at noon on Saba. But Stevanis bought us a warm loaf of bread from his wife's bakery, and drove us about the seven miles of highway to see the sights—tidy houses, goats scattered on near-vertical slopes, the airstrip always compared to the deck of an aircraft carrier, one little gray pet monkey scuttling across the pavement.

A shrewd businessman himself, Stevanis explained that this island, once famous for its seafaring men, now lives on the dole. "Every two weeks, people get a check from the government. It's better than fishin'—nobody drown in the post office!"

Safe anchorage—one of the best in the Caribbean, and surely the prettiest—has made the fame of Antigua, my last landfall in the Leewards. At English Harbour, careful restoration of Nelson's Dockyard has created a fascinating reminder of Nelsonian glory. Yachtsmen arrive in spring to carouse through Sailing Week, while tourists take advantage of direct flights from the U. S. and Europe to the island's sparkling white beaches and azure waters and exceptional hotels. Nancy and I chose a delightful old inn at Nelson's Dockyard, where the dawn cries of doves may rouse you into the illusion that you have sailed backward into history.

In reality, there is promise here for the future. Nancy and I dined at D'Arcy's, a restaurant with good lobster and a fine steel band. The hardworking owner told us that she had sent a daughter through medical school and had a son ready to enter. "They will come back to heal, not stay away to make themselves rich," she said, holding up a graceful, work-worn hand.

For an evening we could relish the present—it was Carnival time. Antigua wisely waits till the end of the tourist season to let loose its own playful soul. My wife and I were the only foreigners in sight when we emerged at dusk from a taxi near the stadium where the most thrilling event would take place: the calypso contest. Under the great lemon globe of the tropic moon, Nancy and I joined the queue awaiting entry, young people dancing and chattering and flirting. All along the dark street, little fires burned beneath grills where plantains and other good things cooked, filling the air with the spicy incense of creole food.

At last we were inside, among tens of thousands in Carnival finery who gave no sign of considering us aliens. A cry of delight that flapped the darkness like a blanket rose from the crowd when the first singer appeared. He gave the people his song:

We are responsible for them children / . . . We must give these children a place within our hearts / They need affection most / Their little lives come first / They are children of the Universe.

A child beside me had been tickling me since we had shared a bottle of pop. She grinned up into my face. It had begun to rain and her cheeks glistened with it, crystalline drops on a darkness finer than velvet.

It was not the rain that wetted my eyes, but the rushing memory of all the goodness I had seen in these islands—goodness which had grown out of the greatest evil that one race has ever visited upon another—and all the hope that has been woven, like a coat of many colors, on historical soil so bitter that a lesser people would long ago have laid down their hoes and burned their boats and stopped their songs.

In the Caribbean night filled with music and cheers, I remembered a woman far down-island. I had asked if she had heard recently from her wandering son. She replied, "By mouth but not by hand. But Noah will land again on this island, his home."

Should no man or woman of these islands ever write me a letter, how I shall have heard from them by mouth, in poetry and song! Here their Ark came to rest, and here they abide.

Veiled by imported lace, 71-year-old Christine Hassell of Saba concentrates on delicate "drawn" or "Spanish work"—distinctive needlework made here since the late 19th century. The woman who introduced the craft learned it from Spanish nuns in Venezuela.

7 | The Virgin Islands

Written by Christine Eckstrom Lee and photographed by Jodi Cobb

Daydream seascapes beneath the waves lure snorkelers to the coral reefs off St. John—one of more than a hundred isles and cays in the Virgin Islands. From wild rain forests to bustling port cities, the islands embrace a medley of landscapes and peoples. Tourism looms large in the Virgins' common future, and close historical and cultural ties bind the islanders, who proudly call their homeland "the place where tired angels pause to rest."

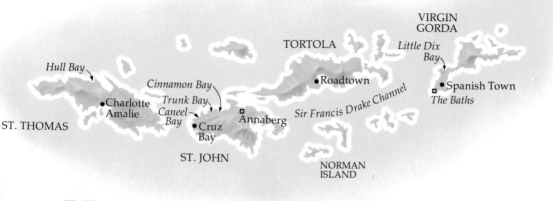

Pirate haunts, pawns of Europe, vacationer's goal: The islands Columbus sighted in 1493 and named for the legendary St. Ursula and her 11,000 Virgins share a past as colorful as the waters that surround them. Six European flags have flown above the mountainous Virgins, which remain politically divided. St. John, St. Thomas, and St. Croix form a United States Territory, and the isles northeast of St. John comprise a British Crown Colony.

ANEGADA

The Settlement●

VIRGIN GORDA

TORTOLA   *Little Dix Bay*

Hull Bay

Cinnamon Bay   ●Roadtown   ●Spanish Town
                                             □ *The Baths*

●Charlotte   *Trunk Bay*
Amalie   *Caneel*   *Sir Francis Drake Channel*
          Bay   □ Annaberg
ST. THOMAS   ●Cruz
              Bay

ST. JOHN

NORMAN ISLAND

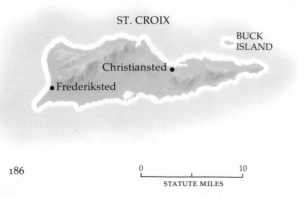

ST. CROIX

BUCK ISLAND

Christiansted ●

●Frederiksted

0   10
STATUTE MILES

igh and green, the profiles of the Virgins rose and fell along the horizon like a school of rollicking sea dragons as the sloop moved among them. Then, stepping ashore on Anegada, I had the sensation of standing on a flatboat lodged on a sandbar.

Northernmost of the cluster of isles and cays known as the Virgin Islands, Anegada bears no resemblance to its neighbors. Its greatest elevation is only 25 feet. Its name, in Spanish, means Drowned One. Its beauty is elemental: wide blue skies, rough shrubs and white sand, a labyrinth of reefs beneath prism-clear waters. Horse Shoe Reef alone has claimed some 200 ships—almost one wreck for every resident today. Here life,

too, is elemental: It centers on the sea.

I sailed to Anegada with Ian Bergman, a young charter skipper working out of Roadtown, Tortola, and we met a man whose life reflects the land—and sea—he has lived on.

Captain Vanterpool makes his home in The Settlement, Anegada's only town. Chickens scurried away, clucking, as we walked to the door where he stood, motioning us inside.

"Come in, come in, come in," he said. "Sit down, sit down." The room measured 9 by 11 feet; it contained nine chairs. "I like to have visitors."

Neatly dressed in a black beret, white shirt, black pants, and white sneakers, he sat, crossed his legs, folded his knotty hands in his lap. "Well," he said, "you must be sailors." Ian said we were. "I'm a man of the sea too." He showed us a card with his picture: James Wallace Vanterpool, Retired Seaman, born 28 November 1891.

"Ah my dear son, I been shipwrecked three times. Three times. Each time the sea deliver me back to Anegada."

He described the wrecks in detail. One ship sank during a hurricane in 1924 that began "when a small cloud make up the size of three tablecloths. Then we hear the rolling, ah my dear son, the sky rolled in. Whoop, there go the main halyard and soon she went down."

His heritage suggests the complex strands that meet in the Virgins. He told us of a grandfather, Captain Arch. "He was a white man; he was a Dutch, and he married the lady named Jane. My father, his eyes were blue as a grape, but that's where we got the color. Then I married a Dutch lady from St. Martin, so I started Dutch and ended Dutch.

"Ah, I almost forgot." He stood up and slipped out for a moment, returning with a gallon jug of deep-purple liquid. "I make this myself." He poured us each a cupful, and smiled as we sipped. The drink was thick and fruity, with a gentle bite. "I use sea grapes, rum, syrup, a little almond, orange peel, vanilla, and ginger. Now one thing is missing. Guess!" At each misguided guess his smile widened.

"Prunes!" he said finally, with delight. "If you don't put prunes, you have no liquor. White folks give it the name cancer cure. They say that's why I live so long. I call it grape wine. Just grape wine. And I say, 'Anegada is why I live so long.' The sea she delivered me up three times, she delivered me back to Anegada."

From his walls, the face of Jesus looks down—Jesus at the Last Supper, Jesus with the fishermen. In parting, our host raised his hand: "Come back, come back, and may the sea treat you well."

Sea and storm have stricken these islands over the years. So have men. Since 1493, when Columbus discovered the group, conquest and colonization, sugar and slavery, have shaped their fate. Today the western isles of St. Thomas, St. John, and St. Croix are a territory of the United States; the eastern isles form a British Crown Colony. But the flags of Spain, England, the Netherlands, France, the Knights of Malta, and Denmark have also fluttered over St. Croix alone. Now the group shares a single major industry—tourism—and with rising numbers of visitors come rising waves of change.

Of the major islands, remote Anegada remains the least developed. Beyond The Settlement lie a few scattered homes, one small hotel, and a pancake wilderness of shrubs. Ian and I drove around with Anthony Smith, who runs the power station, and his son, Launset, a teacher. They showed us a glossy brochure detailing a massive resort.

"The plan failed," said Launset. "The developers extended the airstrip, and built this road. They put in a power station, and started making a harbor. Then they lost their lease."

"Are you glad?" I asked.

Launset laughed. "Yes. Anegada needs improvements, but not too many. We have freedom here. There are no robberies, no murders—no crime. We can live the way we like, go where we want to go. That's why I love Anegada. I have freedom here."

There is still a pioneer quality to life in the British Virgins. In Spanish Town, on Virgin Gorda—an island of a thousand people—I met a woman who served as country doctor to the entire population for thirty-five years. Nurse Iris O'Neal relaxed in a rocking chair on her porch, her hair coiled in neat braids, her voice gentle and lilting.

"Yes, I suppose I helped most of the people on this island into the world," she said. "I had no one to turn to. If there was something I couldn't handle, I had to take the patient in a sailing boat to the hospital on Tortola." That could take three or four hours, and in foul weather it could be dangerous. "Now we have the new clinic." In 1977, when Queen Elizabeth II visited the colony, she inspected Virgin Gorda's modern medical facility: Nurse Iris O'Neal Clinic.

"When I came to Virgin Gorda in 1943, we walked wherever we had to go, or used a horse or donkey. People weren't so well off, but they shared what they had."

Promise of undreamed-of bargains entices cruise-ship passengers to duty-free shops on St. Thomas. When tourism ended in Cuba in 1961, it began to soar in the U. S. Virgins. More than half of their one million visitors each year arrive by cruise ship in St. Thomas's Charlotte Amalie harbor— and promptly rush ashore for a whirlwind day of sun, sights, and shops.

She paused as a small plane roared low overhead. "There isn't as much banding together as there used to be. The young people aren't interested in cultivating and fishing. They see the tourists relaxing and they want to find the easy way, too."

In 1964, Laurance S. Rockefeller completed a resort at Little Dix Bay; since that time, development has grown, slowly. Little Dix is quiet, under-stated, exquisitely landscaped. A number of islanders work there, in a variety of jobs. "Before Little Dix, we had one, maybe two jeeps on the island," recalls Nurse Iris. "Now they are everywhere. There are more jobs. But some of the good qualities have been lost. The quiet-ness. The respect."

She showed me dainty placemats of "drawn work," lacy thread designs filling patterns of squares cut in linen. She learned the skill from her mother, who had learned it from her mother. "I thought before my eyes get too weak, I'll show the little ones how to do this. I want to pass it on. Otherwise, it will die. It's a small thing, but our history is made of these small things."

The early history of the Virgin Islands is sketchy but swashbuckling. Pirates may have been the first Europeans to settle along the shores of Tortola, where palm fronds clacked in the trade winds and sculpted coves sheltered them from open seas and honest eyes. Tales of Francis Drake and John Hawkins, treasures lost and fortunes found, are still current here. The truth is as elusive as the treasure, but on Tortola I met a woman who told me a story. . . .

Jill Tattersall and her husband,

Dreams of a promised land in Africa inspire a growing number of islanders known as the Rastafarians—followers of a back-to-Africa religious movement that has spread out of Jamaica. On the waterfront in Christiansted, a young man wearing the popular "dreadlocks" hairstyle favored by the Rastas relaxes on a bench by an old Danish fort.

Robin, live in a rambling house known as the Purple Palace. It overlooks the harbor of Roadtown, where dozens of sailboats bob in neat rows. Robin, a sailor and a surgeon, uses one wing of the home as his clinic. Jill, author of a dozen historical novels, works in a book-lined corner of a large sitting room. For two years she has been researching her next novel, a saga of a Dutch family's voyage to the New World and their eventual settlement on Tortola.

She told of fitful attempts to colonize by the Dutch, English, French, and Spanish. "Sometimes the news of a war or a peace treaty back home didn't reach the colonists for months. They weren't sure who their enemies were, or what the next ship on the horizon would bring. Just about everyone was a freebooter. They did it to survive.

"Do you know about the Norman Island treasure?"

Norman is a small, unpopulated isle across the Francis Drake Channel from Tortola. Local lore says it inspired Robert Louis Stevenson's *Treasure Island*.

"Normand was a French pirate living on Anegada with other buccaneers, who lured passing ships onto the reefs and plundered them," she said. "One night he took a ship flying the Spanish flag and found so much gold and goods he didn't dare to return to Anegada. He went to what is now Norman to hide his booty. He and his crew buried the dyestuffs and tobacco and supplies, but with a select 'trusty band' he stashed the *real* treasure—chests of gold doubloons.

"As pirates would, he bragged of his deeds. The authorities caught up with him in St. Thomas and executed him.

"*A treasure chest with its lid thrown open, its glittering contents displayed for all to see*"— *the author's words convey the bravura of St. Thomas, commercial hub of the entire group. With an eye on Charlotte Amalie's fine harbor, the U. S. bought the Danish Virgins in 1917 to protect sea lanes to the Panama Canal. Now U. S. and West Indian opportunity-seekers have swelled St. Thomas's population. Visitors hunt for bargains in Charlotte Amalie, where the gleaming lights of cruise ships rival the sparkle of jewels displayed in waterfront shops like Pandora's Box (right).*

Tortolans sneaked over to Norman Island, dug up the dyes and tobacco, but never found the gold.

"It was early in this century when a fisherman from Anegada took shelter from a downpour in a cave on Norman. He noticed a strange pile of stones—too neatly arranged. They concealed a false wall, and behind it lay the treasure. He took the gold and sailed for St. Thomas, never to return to Anegada.

"That fisherman's family is prominent in St. Thomas today, and there are branches of the family throughout the Virgins. They don't really discuss the story. But I met a woman of the family once, and asked her about it. She said, 'Well, I don't know anything for certain. But I'll tell you this. On my wedding day, I wore a necklace of gold doubloons that reached to my knees.'"

Treasure has many guises here. Seekers of solitude find it in secluded coves where the water is soft and cool, where the sun melts into the skin like lotion. Sailors see it in the wind and the sea: steady trades to belly the sails, sheltered channels to cross and recross, scores of little isles to explore. In the British Virgins, the booming business is in charter boats and "bareboats"—those rented, without captain or crew, to experienced sailors only.

Since bareboating reached the area ten years ago, tourism has increased fivefold, to almost 100,000 persons a year. More than half of them rent boats; and perhaps one reason the British Virgins retain their rural charm is that most of the tourists are afloat.

I remember a night I spent on a sloop anchored in calm waters off Anegada. The air was so clean and fresh, like the scent of melting ice, that its very clarity seemed an element I could hold against a dark sky to watch it shine. The weak lights of small houses by the sea dimmed in the brilliance of the stars; but far away a pale glow tinted the southwestern sky, where the lights of St. Thomas whitened the night.

If the British Virgins are a treasure chest hidden in the sand, St. Thomas and the other U. S. islands are a chest with its lid thrown open, its glittering contents on display. Charlotte Amalie—port city for St. Thomas and capital of the U. S. Virgins—is the commercial center for the entire group. While the British islanders count their jeeps, St. Thomas struggles with traffic jams.

Streets in Charlotte Amalie are bustling, lined with shops and restaurants that reveal a pastiche of cultures: Danish stonework and brickwork, Spanish arches, ornate French balconies, English carved wood. In the shops, goods are duty-free—as they have been since 1755, when the Danes made St. Thomas a free port. Activity has centered on the harbor ever since; and in the past two decades, cruise ships have brought a new wealth to island economy. A large ship carries enough people to triple the population of Anegada, and most of them rush ashore to the shops to browse and buy. Arriving by sea or by air, more than one million tourists visit the U. S. Virgins each year.

Moreover, the resident population has more than tripled since 1960, passing 100,000. U. S. "continentals," Puerto Ricans, and West Indians from other islands have come in search of an easier life, or the off-chance of a job. Inevitably, there are signs of strain.

One night on St. Thomas I watched the competition for Junior Calypso King of the 1979 Carnival. The Mighty Spear sang of the frustrations of living among crowds: "Please leave me alone / Let me have my home / I cannot live with everyone / So please leave me alone. . . ." The Mighty Midget sang "Oh gone, Oh gone, the light's gone out again." This drew cheers, for St. Thomas suffers constant shortages of water and power. "There's too many people on this tiny little island," I was told time and again.

Still, there are communities with strong ties to the past, proud of their

"We come forward to teach His word," says Rastafarian Nigeria Bramada, pausing with his family by a St. Thomas home. Followers of this movement live on St. Thomas and St. Croix, with a faith one writer calls "an alternative spiritual nationality."

cultural unity. One such group is the Frenchies, farmers and fishermen who came from St. Barts in the mid-18th century to settle on St. Thomas's north shore and by the harbor. The first were two brothers named LaPlace; and one afternoon I talked with fisherman Pete LaPlace at his home above Hull Bay.

Coral, sea fans, and shells filled neat rows of shelves that lined the walls of the living room. "The ocean is my life," said Pete. "When I am on the sea, I am free. It's me and my boat and the sea. She feed me, she take care of me, and I'm happy, yes!" At 45, Pete is sturdy and muscular, with a raspy laugh and an earthy humor. He spoke of the French with pride, boasting of the beauty of French women and the great size of French families.

On his wall is a plaque that the terri-

torial government awarded to him and his stepson Ralph. In 1977 a small plane crashed into the sea near their boat, and they rescued its eight passengers. They lost their seine—worth a year's earnings—but all the victims survived.

Not long before the crash, said Pete, a strange thing had happened. "I went free diving, and I suddenly felt a weight on my shoulder. It comes to me as a young lady with a child in her arms. I say, 'Relax, Pete, the pressure got to you, man.' I pass my hand but it's not there. But the feeling is there, trying to tell me something. The following week we rescued the plane in the same area. Right away I realized why the woman was sitting on my shoulder.

"A week or two later, the woman is back. I say, 'Ah! What now!' I have the feeling *(Continued on page 208)* 193

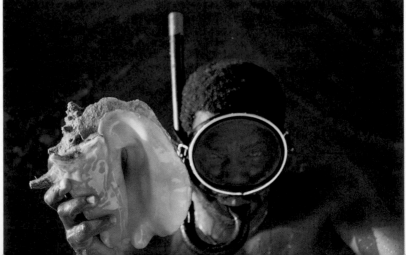

INA BLOOK

W*here pleasure means business for just about everyone, pellucid waters and soothing trade winds provide the Virgin Islands' greatest natural resources. Sunlight marbles the shallows off St. John as a lifeguard takes a dip in Trunk Bay (above, left)—part of St. John's 5,650 undersea acres protected as a national park. Nearby, off Cinnamon Bay, a fresh breeze tightens the sails of the ketch Malabar Cay. Sailors treasure the gentle waters encircled by the Virgins, and in recent years charter-boat businesses have boomed. Islanders look to the sea for food and livelihood. A sailing skipper and a fisherman, born on Anguilla, Albert "Abu" Connor (left) takes tourists to St. Croix's offshore reefs—and dives for conch, a Caribbean delicacy prepared in fritters, salads, and stews.*

Monument to the heyday of King Sugar survives at St. John's Annaberg mill, once a working sugar factory. Rollers inside the plantation windmill (above) crushed juice from cane for sugar, molasses, and rum. A hundred plantations once covered St. John's hilly land; they thrived until 1733, when most of the island's Danish planters died in a bloody slave uprising. The sugar economy waned; Denmark abolished slavery in 1848; and St. John fell into a century-long slumber. Then, in 1956, conservationist Laurance S. Rockefeller donated more than 5,000 acres for a national park that now protects three-fourths of the island as well as offshore waters. In 1952 he had acquired a resort property on Caneel Bay—"far more beautiful than its brochures," says the author—near the island's west end. The parkland surrounding Caneel Bay also embraces Annaberg's ruins, lush forests, and powdery beaches like Trunk Bay (right) as a legacy for the future.

Ranching's a family affair for the Lawaetzes of St. Croix, gathered at their homestead near the island's west end. Born under the Danish flag, a member of the territorial senate for 20 years, Frits E. Lawaetz (above) with two of his sons manages Annaly Farms, a 5,500-acre property in the western hills. They raise Senepol cattle—a local breed developed for the tropical Caribbean—and sell the beef to Virgin Island markets. At left, Annaly Farms cowboys Juan Ponce and Jonathan Hitesman drive cattle across a pasture to the dip tank.

*J*oy of racing draws bettors to St. Croix's Flamboyant Race Track for a pastime as popular in the Virgins as in islands to the south. Below, Bold Hessian, a five-year-old Crucian Thoroughbred, gets expert preparation for his race in the 1978 Pre-Holidays Open Classic; trainer Hasseen Iles beams a confident smile. At right, Bold Hessian thunders down the stretch to victory over off-island rivals. At the fence, a spectator studies his program—too young to place his bet, but quite old enough to follow the form of bloodlines and stables, trainers and jockeys.

Backwater beauty sets the tone of the British Virgins, where life takes an easy gait. On Virgin Gorda, Ingrid Sprauve and Franklin Penn, both age 10, play with a dog in Spanish Town. Below, Larry Turnbull, 8, strolls along a ridge on Tortola, largest of the British Virgins and home to most of their 13,000 residents. When the islands' sugar economy went stagnant in the 19th century and land values fell, tracts of the old estates came into the hands of former slaves. Their descendants now own, or lease from the Crown, more than half the land in the colony—and cling to it proudly.

Preceding pages: Beyond Virgin Gorda, the British and U. S. isles sprinkle a sun-glazed western horizon. Only Anegada and St. Croix lie too distant to be seen.

*A*way-from-it-all settings fringe the island of Virgin Gorda, where vacationers shed city cares and relax in the transparent waters of coves like Little Dix Bay (below), at a resort opened by Laurance Rockefeller in 1964. At the island's southwestern tip lies the Virgins' most dramatic rock formation, The Baths. Beneath boulders three stories high, snorkelers don their gear to explore the shallow pools that wind through sunlit grottoes. At right, the hills of Tortola roll along the horizon beyond charter boats anchored off The Baths. "I love the colors here," Virgin Islands artist Paul Youngblood told the author. "They're so vibrant and wild—it's impossible to exaggerate! Every day I see something beautiful."

that again I have something big to do."

Not long after, Pete helped found the Virgin Islands Federation of Fishermen, to unite the people in the local industry and lobby for fishermen's rights. "I don't feel the woman on my shoulder no more," he said. "We're winning the fight. The government is changing the policies to help the fishermen—all the Virgin Islands fishermen. The British ones on Tortola too. They're our brothers, yes! Some people say, 'But he's black.' I say, 'He's black, so what. I can't help that, he's got to eat too.'

"The Virgin Islands is like a fiction movie, yes! All the luxury, the money. It comes in and it's gone. We're not used to the luxury we have here now. We got to make a contribution. My father left me something good, yes! We have to leave something for our children and our grandchildren or they will have nothing. We have to live for now and fight for today, yes! We will win."

I thought of Pete's omens as I waited in predawn blackness on a pier in Frenchtown for fishermen I would join that day: Women on fishing boats are considered unlucky if not dangerous, but Reynaldo "Manta" Turbe had agreed to take me out on his 32-foot prowler, *Dee-Dee*. Traditionally, Frenchies fish alone in small open boats and haul in their fish pots by hand—a grueling, risky occupation. Manta's boat is larger, letting him set more pots, and he uses a power winch to haul them in. "It's a hard life," he said, "and in a way I've made it easier."

We headed south ten miles to the edge of the continental shelf, toward St. Croix. The swells ran eight feet high; the boat rose and pitched; squalls showered us and passed on.

For six hours that day, Manta and his mate "Dak" hauled in traps and set new ones. Most held some grouper; none were full. "The catch is unpredictable in the new moon," Manta said. But when we got back and people eyed our little pile of fish, one woman stared at me and said pointedly, "A bad catch."

In recent years, a new group has appeared in the Virgins. Its members are the young black islanders who call themselves the Rastafarians, and they are most easily recognized by their hair, worn in uncombed "dreadlocks." Some people fear them, or blame them for the rising crime rate in the U.S. islands. No doubt there are those who affect the style of the Rastas but fail to adopt their beliefs. The movement is essentially peaceful; and from its beginnings in Jamaica it has spread through the Caribbean since the 1950's. On St. Croix, along the Mahogany Road that winds through lush rain forest, I met the leader of a small Rasta community, a man called Lumumba.

As I waited for him in a roadside hut, a tune stirred in my mind. The beat was reggae, the throbbing, driving music that developed in Jamaica. The lyrics stemmed from Psalm 137. "By the rivers of Babylon, / Where he sat down, / And there he went / When he remembered Zion. / But the wicked carried us away, captivity / Require from us a song, / How can we sing King Alfa song / In a strange land."

"This is Babylon," said Lumumba, "and Africa is Zion. We are the sons of Ham, we were brought here against our will, and we must return to Africa." He came in barefoot and barechested, lean and trim in simple cotton trousers. Lumumba flashes warm smiles as he speaks, and punctuates his sentences with "You check?" and "Check it." I could easily see him as a leader.

"I am from Dominica," he said. "Two of my grandparents were Caribs. For seven years I lived in New York and made money, you check? Then I realized I had lost myself. I was corrupted. What profiteth it a man to gain the world and lose his soul? So I came here. This is our repatriation camp. We will go to Africa."

He pointed to the walls of the hut. "See this? You won't find a nail in it. See its shape? Round like the way the wind flows. The wind can't blow this down because it's shaped like the wind. This is the way our ancestors lived, and when we go to Africa this is how we will live. We are not West Indians, we are Africans." Gooseflesh appears on his skin when he says "Africa."

"I traveled in the U. S. south, and there I learned racism, you check? I was hassled. The U. S. uses prejudice to keep people apart; it makes no sense. The U. S. will fall like Babylon." He paced the hut. "Why are men unkind to each other? Think of the wild horses, how they run free. Why can't man run free as the horse? I want to go to Africa. I want to see the jungle." He smiled, and spoke in a joyous whisper: "I want to see the lions!"

He and his group sell handmade craftwork to finance the trip to Africa. The baskets are patient and exquisite, the fabric prints wild and colorful, the bowls rough-hewn and handsome. Several times I saw taxis filled with tourists pause in the road. Faces peered through rolled-up windows, cameras pressed against the glass, hands tapped the driver's shoulder, and the cab moved on. When one car stopped, Lumumba called, "Come on in! We're friendly! This is real native culture here!" But a hand tapped the driver, and the car moved on.

On the northern coast of St. Croix lies Christiansted, with 5,400 people making it the island's largest town. Crisscrossed with brick and stone streets lined with pastel buildings—many preserved as national historic sites—Christiansted reflects 184 years of orderly Danish rule. When the United States purchased its islands from Denmark in 1917 for $25,000,000—at $300 an acre, the highest price ever paid for U. S. land—most of the acreage came with St. Croix. From its desert-dry east to its western rain forest, its terrain is the most varied in the Virgins. And a few miles from Christiansted lies the most unusual attraction: an underwater national monument off Buck Island.

Aboard the sloop *Intrepid*, I sailed with Anton Teytaud to the Buck Island reefs. With snorkels and flippers we explored a world of intense colors and bizarre shapes unrivaled by anything known on land. "I do this every day," said Anton. "It's never the same—the sea is always different, every day something changes."

Anton's heritage is Danish, Dutch, and Venezuelan. He has lived on St. Croix all his life; although he has grandchildren, he seems at once youthful and ageless. He told me of changes within the last ten years—"so many tourists, so many newcomers. The young people don't want to work the land. They are restless and frustrated. Now we have racial tension, and so much crime. There is no one cause. Our roots are here, we want to stay, but we may be forced to leave if conditions don't improve."

Anton is writing a book about his childhood here, and in 1974 he published a collection of short plays entitled *Sarah and Addie*. His heroines are Crucian market women who gossip and comment on the state of things. Performed on the stage or broadcast over the radio, their dialogue has delighted islanders and tourists alike.

One play focuses on the jewelry made with old bits of china and seen in shops around the islands. A tourist wearing a china brooch buys a bunch of Sarah's bananas. When the woman leaves, Sarah identifies the ornament as "a piece of ah ole chamber pot wha ah had . . . wha had geh bruk from me an I had pitch it behine de fowl house in de yard."

Addie: "NO SARAH, YO JOKIN'!"

Sarah: " . . . Ah mus know it, tis under me bed it been fo years! . . . Well me sweet peace, and the soul wearin it so proud on she bosom!"

Addie has a question: "Wha yo tink she would say ef she know?"

"Ah dunno me dear marm," says

*S*t. *Croix's warm seas shelter a fragile playground, habitat of creatures like the dainty sea horse above and myriad fishes and corals. Off the northeast shore, a snorkeler explores Buck Island's reefs, an underwater national monument. Efforts to protect the reef ecosystems have their counterpart on land, as Virgin Islanders defend cherished traditions against the pressures of change. Their courtesy finds warm expression in the words of a venerable seaman on Anegada: "Come back, come back, and may the sea treat you well."*

Sarah. "But it have sarve me well, an ah glad to see piece ah it fall into such good hands."

Sarah's satisfaction would fit the fortunes of St. John. Set like a jagged green jewel between St. Thomas and Tortola, St. John is the quintessential Virgin—unspoiled and serene. It will remain so. Conservationist Laurance S. Rockefeller began purchasing land in the early 1950's and donated 5,000 acres for a national park. Since then the park has grown to encompass three-fourths of the island and thousands of acres of the surrounding seafloor.

With Park Ranger Noble Samuel—a St. Johnian highly knowledgeable about the island's flora and fauna—I spent a day exploring the forest trails and paradise beaches of a land whose atmosphere relaxes the spirit like a smile.

We went snorkeling at Trunk Bay, now part of this underwater national park, and Noble dived to a cluster of ominous black sea urchins resting near a forest of elkhorn coral. He swept his hand near one; it bounced up like tumbleweed, and he let it drift onto his open palm. When he brought it to rest on my hand, the spines tickled like blunt toothpicks and I lost my fear—but not my respect—for the creature.

Late in the afternoon, we explored the ruins of an old sugar mill at Annaberg. As we descended a trail to the parking lot, we met four tourists who stopped us with questions about the ruins. Noble answered them, and glanced at the lot, where the tourists' driver waited by his van. "Who is your driver?" Noble asked. They seemed puzzled; they said they didn't know.

"You mean you been riding around all day with this man and you don't even know his name?" No one spoke.

Then one woman looked at Noble and said, "You're right." She nodded her head: "You're absolutely right." She walked down the trail toward the driver, and I saw him smile as she approached and extended her hand to his.

Contributors

A native Floridian, NATHAN BENN worked for the *Miami Herald* and *Palm Beach Post-Times* while studying at the University of Miami. After graduating in 1972, he became a contract photographer for NATIONAL GEOGRAPHIC. His work for Special Publications has included subjects as diverse as medicinal plants in Africa and Asia, Biblical archaeology, and ethnic minorities in the United States. Today he lives in Washington, D. C.

National Geographic Photographer JODI COBB joined the Society's staff in 1977 after free-lance assignments ranging from California to Plains, Georgia. Since 1968 her career has included teaching. Her work has appeared in varied publications as well as exhibitions, winning numerous awards; this book marks her first coverage for Special Publications. She grew up in Iran, lived for a time in Texas, and received bachelor's and master's degrees in journalism from the University of Missouri.

Since 1975 photographer COTTON COULSON has worked under contract with the National Geographic Society, with assignments as varied as Oregon and Estonia. A landsman by preference, he found the Grenadines easier sailing than the North Atlantic, where he photographed the leather boat *Brendan*. A New Yorker born, he graduated from New York University and now lives in Washington, D. C.

Associate Editor of the Special Publications and School Services Division, DONALD J. CRUMP supervises picture editing, layout, and design for books, educational filmstrips, and *World* magazine. A native Oklahoman who graduated from Oklahoma State, he worked on newspapers before his graduate study at the University of Missouri School of Journalism. During the Korean Conflict he served as an officer in the U. S. Air Force. He joined the NATIONAL GEOGRAPHIC staff as a picture editor in 1961; in 1965 he helped launch the Special Publications series, which reaches its 56th volume with this book.

TOR EIGELAND lived for a year in Trinidad after university study in Canada and Mexico, then began his career in free-lance photojournalism. For Special Publications he has had assignments in the Sudan, Australia, Europe, Texas, and Mexico, writing about the Tarahumara Indians in *Primitive Worlds* and the Italian ranges in *The Alps*. Norwegian by birth, now a U. S. citizen, he makes his home in Spain.

Before coming to the Society in 1958, MARY ANN HARRELL earned a B.A. in English at Wellesley College and an M.A. at the University of North Carolina (her native state). She wrote a historical account of the Supreme Court in *Equal Justice Under Law*, produced by the Society as a public service. Assignments for Special Publications have taken her to East Africa, Australia, and South Pacific islands.

CHRISTINE ECKSTROM LEE received her bachelor's degree in English from Mount Holyoke College and joined the Society's staff in 1974; two years later she began writing for Special Publications. She reported on the Minoan civilization for *Mysteries of the Ancient World* and the Adirondacks for *Exploring America's Backcountry*. A native of Philadelphia, she now lives in Arlington, Virginia.

A frequent contributor to NATIONAL GEOGRAPHIC, free lance CHARLES McCARRY rode the Mormons' Honeymoon Trail for the Special Publication *Trails West*. The most recent of his four novels is *The Better Angels;* his most recent nonfiction is *Double Eagle,* an account of the first successful transatlantic crossing by balloon. He lives in his native Massachusetts.

As a young lieutenant on an old destroyer, BART McDOWELL first traversed the Caribbean for the U. S. Navy in World War II. He became a writer for NATIONAL GEOGRAPHIC in 1957; today he is an assistant editor. He is author of four Special Publications: *The Revolutionary War, Gypsies, The American Cowboy,* and *Journey Across Russia: The Soviet Union Today*. He graduated from the University of California, with advanced study at other universities including Missouri's School of Journalism.

Acknowledgments

The Special Publications Division is grateful to the persons and organizations portrayed, named, or quoted in this book for their generous cooperation and assistance during its preparation, and also to many others. Embassy staff and other government officials of the Caribbean countries have helped immeasurably, as have specialists at the Sint Eustatius Historical Foundation and the University of the West Indies, the Inter-American Foundation, the National Meteorological Center (NOAA), and the Smithsonian Institution.

Dr. Robert L. Carneiro and Dr. Warren Morrill gave expert advice on details. John H. McCashion identified and dated the pipes pictured on page 166.

Professor Sidney W. Mintz of the Johns Hopkins University has kindly served as overall consultant.

Innumerable individuals of the islands—notably including hotel personnel and schoolchildren— have aided this project. Among them: Anthony W. N. Alleyne, Phyllis and Robert Allfrey, Carl and Janice Armour, Paul Backshall, Judy Ballangee, Carolyn Barrow, Hon. Errol Barrow, Noel and Mary Bevan, Pamela Biolley, Danny Bridges, Gabriel Charles, Joseph Davelyn DeCouteau, Frank da Silva, David and Betty Edgecombe, Joseph E. Edmunds, Richard S. Fiske, Timberlake Foster, Hilary Frederick, Michael Gilkes, Harry and Barbara Goodheart, E. G. B. Gooding, Winston and Janet Govia, Art Hansen, Lennox Honychurch, Richard A. Howard, Geoffrey Irons, Errol John-Baptiste, Helena Jones, Cuthbert Julien, Edwin Laurent, Larry and Liz Leighton, Alison Rees Mabry, Woodville Marshall, Atherton Martin, Georgina Masson, D. L. Matheson, Christopher Maximé, Samuel P. McChesney, Harold McKell, Bob Neymeyer, Martin Norman, Ilma O'Neal, Carol and Cedric Osborne, Heather and Anscele Payne, Nora Peacocke, Ellen Peters, Sara Polk, Donald Roch, Stella St. John, Charles Savarin, Lawson Sergeant, Keith Simmons, Rickey Singh, Barbara Station, Hilary E. Wattley.

Index

Boldface indicates illustrations; *italic*
refers to picture legends (captions)

Library of Congress CIP Data
Isles of the Caribbean.
  Bibliography: p.
  Includes index.
  1. Antilles, Lesser—Description and travel.   I. National Geographic Society, Washington, D. C. Special Publications Division.
F2001.I79   972.9   78-61266
ISBN 0-87044-274-0

Additional Reading

The reader may wish to consult the *National Geographic Index* for related articles. To supplement the numerous guidebooks and travel narratives, the following may also be useful.

History: Ypie Attema, *St. Eustatius;* Sir Alan Burns, *History of the British West Indies;* Raymund P. Devas, *A History of the Island of Grenada, 1498-1796;* Howard A. Fergus, *History of Alliouagana [Montserrat]*; Jerome S. Handler, *The Unappropriated People;* Johan Hartog, *Geschiedenis van de Nederlandse Antillen* and, in English, local histories; Lennox Honychurch, *The Dominica Story;* F. A. Hoyos, *Barbados;* C. L. R. James, *Beyond a Boundary;* C. Jesse, *Outlines of St. Lucia's History;* Sir Arthur Lewis, *Labour in the West Indies;* Gordon K. Lewis, *The Growth of the Modern West Indies;* Samuel Eliot Morison, *Admiral of the Ocean Sea;* V. S. Naipaul, *The Loss of El Dorado;* Linda S. Newson, *Aboriginal and Spanish Colonial Trinidad;* J. H. Parry and Philip Sherlock, *A Short History of the West Indies;* Eric Williams, *From Columbus to Castro, The History of the Caribbean 1492-1969* and *History of the People of Trinidad and Tobago.*

Geography and area studies: Jan Knippers Black et al., *Area Handbook for Trinidad and Tobago;* Helmut Blume, *The Caribbean Islands;* Sidney E. Chernick et al., *The Commonwealth Caribbean;* Irene Hawkins, *The Changing Face of the Caribbean;* David Lowenthal, *West Indian Societies;* Claudio Véliz, ed., *Latin America and the Caribbean.*

Yachting: Donald M. Street, Jr., *A Cruising Guide to the Lesser Antilles.*

Literature: Timothy Callender, *It So Happen* and *The Watchman;* Aimé Césaire, *Cahier d'un retour au pays natal* (tr. John Berger and Anna Bostock, *Return to My Native Land*); Austin C. Clarke, *The Survivors of the Crossing;* John Figueroa, ed., *Caribbean Voices;* C. L. R. James, *Minty Alley;* Lilyan Kesteloot, *Black Writers in French;* George Lamming, *In the Castle of My Skin;* Earl Lovelace, *The Schoolmaster;* Paule Marshall, *The Chosen Place, the Timeless People;* Ian McDonald, *The Humming-bird Tree;* V. S. Naipaul, *A House for Mr. Biswas;* H. Orlando Patterson, *The Children of Sisyphus;* Andrew Salkey, ed., *Caribbean Essays* and *West Indian Stories;* Samuel Selvon, *A Brighter Sun;* Derek Walcott, *Dream on Monkey Mountain* and *The Star-apple Kingdom;* John Wickham, *Casuarina Row.*

Composition for ISLES OF THE CARIBBEAN by National Geographic's Photographic Services, Carl M. Shrader, Chief; Lawrence F. Ludwig, Assistant Chief. Printed and bound by Holladay-Tyler Printing Corp., Rockville, Md. Color separations by the Lanman Companies, Washington, D. C.; Graphic South, Charlotte, N.C.; National Bickford Graphics, Inc., Providence, R.I.; Progressive Color Corp., Rockville, Md.; The J. Wm. Reed Co., Alexandria, Va.